Prep-Ahead

BREAKFASTS

&

LUNCHES

Prep-Ahead BREAKFASTS & LUNCHES

75 NO-FUSS RECIPES TO SAVE YOU TIME & MONEY

Alea Milham

AUTHOR OF *PREP-AHEAD MEALS FROM SCRATCH*

PAGE STREET
PUBLISHING CO.

PAGE STREET
PUBLISHING CO.

Copyright © 2018 Alea Milham

First published in 2018 by
Page Street Publishing Co.
27 Congress Street, Suite 105
Salem, MA 01970
www.pagestreetpublishing.com

Distributed by Macmillan, sales in Canada by The Canadian Manda Group.

22   21   20   19   18   1   2   3   4   5

ISBN-13: 978-1-62414-562-9
ISBN-10: 1-62414-562-0

Library of Congress Control Number: 2017959747

Cover and book design by Page Street Publishing Co.
Photography by Ken Goodman

Printed and bound in China

In loving memory of my sister,
CORRIEDAWN GREILING.

Contents

INTRODUCTION

There are many books dedicated to making quick and easy dinners. In fact, my first cookbook, *Prep-Ahead Meals from Scratch*, was devoted to that cause. The concept of prep-ahead cooking makes sense because we don't have a lot of time to spend cooking in the evenings—we are all looking for ways to save time. But if our time is limited in the evenings, it often means we have even less time to devote to cooking in the mornings and none at lunchtime.

We often see mention of athletes and fitness gurus prepping their meals for the week. We look closer at the article because it seems like a good idea, but then we see five days of broiled chicken breasts and think, "That's okay. I'll pass." Just because we don't want to eat plain broiled chicken breasts for lunch five days a week doesn't mean we can't use some of the same meal-prep techniques to create flavorful meals for ourselves and our family.

My family eased into make-ahead breakfasts first. I started by making a couple of batches of muffins on the weekend because I found it convenient to have muffins on hand for an easy breakfast or a quick snack. Then my father-in-law passed the family waffle maker down to my husband. My husband is an "if a little is good, a lot is better" kind of guy and started making a double batch of waffles every other weekend. Having delicious homemade waffles in the freezer that I could prepare in minutes completely hooked me on the idea of make-ahead breakfasts and I encouraged my husband to add pancakes to his weekend repertoire. My husband did, but he took it one step further: he invited the kids to help him. He would quote "Humpty Dumpty" as he broke the eggs, and meal prep became a fun family activity instead of a weekly chore.

Our first make-ahead lunches came about because my oldest son did not like eating leftovers for lunch. Interestingly, he didn't mind eating the same foods we had for dinner as long as they were presented in a different manner. So if I served him tacos for lunch the day after I served tacos for dinner, he would object; but I could take the leftovers from taco night and create a taco salad or a taco rice bowl and he would happily eat them. It wasn't entirely logical, but I am intelligent enough to know not to try to reason with a young child. By accommodating him, I made a discovery: the leftovers stretched much further if I used them to create a different meal. We may have had enough leftover taco fixings for only a couple tacos, but if I used those same ingredients to create individual salads or rice bowls, they stretched to make lunches for the entire family. The concept for my blog, Premeditated Leftovers, was born because with every dinner I made, I was thinking of a creative way to use the leftovers in lunches the next day. As my kids grew and the leftovers became scarcer, I started making a few extra dishes on the weekend that could be used in lunches throughout the week.

In this cookbook, I am sharing easy and delicious make-ahead recipes for breakfast and lunch. These simple dishes will make you look forward to eating a homemade breakfast and packed lunch rather than grabbing packaged food or eating takeout.

Alea

CREATING YOUR OWN CONVENIENCE FOODS

Start by looking at what convenience foods are you buying now that you could easily make ahead of time. For the price of a box of frozen pancakes, you can make a month's worth of pancakes in your kitchen. Instead of buying frozen rice bowls, you can easily make your own versions by doubling a few of your favorite dinner recipes and portioning the leftovers in individual containers over rice. Cooking your breakfasts and lunches in advance will save you money and give you complete control over the ingredients, so you know your dishes are made with ingredients you can feel good about.

ORGANIZING A MEAL-PREP DAY

Some people will be able to do as we did and fit batch-cooking and meal prep into their daily lives. Some of you are so busy you barely have time to sit down, much less think about cooking a week's worth of meals. However, the less time you have, the more important it is to carve out an hour or two on a day off to do some batch-cooking and meal prep. You will feel better and perform better when you are consuming regular meals made from wholesome ingredients.

COME UP WITH A MEAL PLAN

This doesn't have to be overly complicated. Decide how many meals you need to make in advance and multiply that number by how many servings you need for each meal. If there are four people in your family and you need to make breakfasts and lunches for the weekdays, you need enough food to provide twenty breakfasts and twenty lunches. That sounds like a lot, but there are a number of breakfast recipes in this book that make twelve servings and a number of lunch recipes that serve eight. So if you simply make two breakfast recipes and three lunch recipes, you will have enough meals to get you through the week and still provide a little variety.

MAKE YOUR SHOPPING LIST

After you finalize your meal plan, check your pantry, freezer and refrigerator to see which ingredients you already have available, and then create a shopping list for the needed items. Some people find it easier to do their grocery shopping the day before they plan to do their cooking. I prefer to do it the same day. I start washing and prepping produce as I remove it from the grocery bags.

IDENTIFY HOW YOU ARE GOING TO STORE YOUR COOKED FOOD

Will you be placing a batch of muffins in a large freezer bag because you have time to eat at home or do you need them in individual bags so you can eat on the go? Are you going to leave your pre-made salad in the bowl you used to make it in, or are you going to store it as individual servings so they are ready to be added directly to your lunch bags? If you will be storing your food in individual portions, make sure the containers are washed, dried and ready to be filled before you start cooking.

BATCH-PREP INGREDIENTS

Look for common ingredients in the recipes you are going to make to see if some of the ingredients can be prepped together. For example, chop all of the onion at one time and measure it out for the different recipes. You can chop all of your vegetables at one time, then put away the cutting board and start cooking your recipes.

BATCH-COOK COMMON INGREDIENTS

When several recipes call for the same ingredient, you can save time and effort by batch-cooking it. For example, if a couple recipes call for cooked quinoa, cook all of the quinoa needed at the same time. After the quinoa is cooked, divide it up between the recipes calling for it.

Coordinate which appliances you will use for the maximum efficiency. Do two recipes need to be cooked in the oven? Assemble those recipes one after the other, so they can either be cooked at the same time or back-to-back.

MONEY-SAVING GROCERY TIPS

You will save money by cooking your own meals rather than buying packaged foods or eating out, but there are things you can do to save even more on your make-ahead meals.

- Always check out the sales flyer before you shop. It is easier than ever to find what is on sale at your local grocery store because stores now post their weekly sales online. Most grocery stores also have apps where you can find instant in-store coupons.

- You will save on produce by shopping for in-season produce. Not only is it at the peak of freshness but it is also less expensive. If you want to use a fruit or vegetable that is not in season, buy it from the frozen food section. Frozen produce is not only less expensive when buying out-of-season fruits and vegetables but it was frozen shortly after being picked, so it often tastes better than imported out-of-season produce.

- Create your meal plan around the food staples that are on sale and the produce that is in season.

- Stock up on shelf-stable items and freezable items that you regularly use when they are on sale.

- Shop in the bulk section for staples. You will find great deals on grains, beans, flours, nuts and spices in the bulk-bin section of your grocery store.

- Make your own spice mixes, dressings and sauces. Most of the items come together in just a few minutes. In the Pantry Staples section (page 188), you will find recipes for making these items from scratch.

Part 1

MAKE-AHEAD BREAKFASTS

In my family, we all have very different ideas about what constitutes the perfect breakfast. My oldest son loves eggs and breakfast sandwiches. My youngest son prefers waffles and pancakes. Both boys love sausage. My daughter likes overnight refrigerator oatmeal. I prefer hot oatmeal or baked oatmeal. And my husband is a granola-with-yogurt kind of guy. The great thing about make-ahead breakfasts is that we can all enjoy our favorite breakfast foods with minimal work and time in the morning.

Chapter 1

SIMPLE EGG DISHES AND BREAKFAST SANDWICHES

Cooked egg dishes keep quite well. Eggs can be cooked in large batches and either refrigerated for up to three days or frozen for up to one month.

Before freezing a dish that contains eggs, allow it to cool completely. Individually wrap egg cups, egg puffs and egg bowls. You can place plastic wrap over an egg casserole to help prevent ice crystals from forming.

It is best to thaw frozen egg dishes overnight in the refrigerator. If you don't have time for that, you can place the container holding the cooked eggs in a pan of cold water on the counter. The eggs will thaw within 30 to 60 minutes in the pan of water. I have shared tips for reheating frozen eggs in the microwave after each recipe, but that method should be used only when you don't have time for one of the longer thawing methods.

Wrap each breakfast sandwich individually in plastic wrap, parchment paper or foil. Label the sandwiches and add the date. Then place the wrapped sandwiches in a sealable freezer bag or sealable container.

Thaw the sandwiches in the refrigerator overnight if possible. If thawing overnight is not an option, follow the directions in the recipe to thaw them in the microwave. Reheat the breakfast sandwiches on a paper towel or a microwave-safe plate in the microwave. If you like a crisper sandwich and have access to a toaster oven, reheat the sandwiches in a toaster oven for 1 to 2 minutes, or until they are heated through.

Serves 12

BATCH-COOKED, OVEN-BAKED SCRAMBLED EGGS

Baking scrambled eggs in the oven is an easy way to cook a lot of eggs at one time. You can then serve the scrambled eggs as they are or use them in a wrap or breakfast bowl.

INGREDIENTS

12 large eggs

⅓ cup (80 ml) milk

⅓ cup (45 g) diced onion

½ tsp garlic powder

¼ tsp Seasoned Salt (page 191)

¼ tsp coarsely ground pepper

½ cup (60 g) shredded cheddar cheese (optional)

DIRECTIONS

Preheat the oven to 350°F (177°C). Grease a 9 x 13-inch (23 x 33-cm) baking dish.

Add the eggs to a medium bowl. Beat until the eggs turn a light yellow. Add the milk, onion, garlic powder, Seasoned Salt and pepper to the eggs. Whisk until fully incorporated. Stir in the cheddar if desired.

Pour the egg mixture into the greased baking dish.

Bake for 10 minutes. Loosen the eggs from the bottom and sides of the pan, then bake for 5 to 10 minutes, or until the eggs are cooked through.

STORING AND REHEATING

Store the scrambled eggs in a sealed container in the refrigerator for up to 3 days or in the freezer for up to 3 months. Thaw frozen eggs in the refrigerator overnight.

To reheat, place the scrambled eggs on a microwave-safe dish and cook on high for 20 seconds.

BATCH-COOKED
MASON JAR EGGS

Don't have egg rings? No problem. A widemouthed Mason jar lid creates perfectly sized cooked eggs to go on an English muffin!

INGREDIENTS

12 large eggs

⅓ cup (80 ml) milk

⅓ cup (45 g) diced onion

½ tsp garlic powder

¼ tsp Seasoned Salt (page 191)

¼ tsp coarsely ground pepper

½ cup (60 g) shredded cheddar cheese (optional)

DIRECTIONS

Add the eggs to a medium bowl and beat until they turn a light yellow. Add the milk, onion, garlic powder, Seasoned Salt and pepper to the eggs. Whisk until fully incorporated. Stir in the cheddar if desired.

Heat a large skillet over medium heat and grease 12 widemouthed canning jar lids.

Place a lid, top-side up, in the skillet. Using a pot holder, hold down the canning ring as your pour the egg mixture in it. Continue holding the ring down for a couple seconds until the egg just begins to set. Repeat this process with the rest of the egg mixture and jar lids.

Allow the eggs to cook until they are firm and the bottoms begin to brown, approximately 4 to 5 minutes. Lift the lids off the eggs, flip the eggs over and allow them to continue cooking until they are cooked through, approximately 1 to 2 minutes.

STORING AND REHEATING

Store the eggs in a sealed container in the refrigerator for up to 3 days.

To freeze, place the eggs between layers of parchment paper to keep them from sticking. Store them in a sealed container in the freezer for up to 1 month. Thaw frozen eggs in the refrigerator overnight.

To reheat a thawed Mason jar egg, unwrap it, place it on a microwave-safe plate and microwave on high for 20 seconds.

BATCH-COOKED
SHEET PAN EGGS

This is an easy way to batch-cook eggs for a crowd or to fill your freezer with breakfast sandwiches. This is the method used in my Chipotle Egg Muffin Sandwiches (page 32) and Cajun Egg Croissant Sandwiches (page 35).

INGREDIENTS

12 large eggs

½ cup (120 ml) milk

⅓ cup (45 g) diced onion

1 tsp garlic powder

½ tsp Seasoned Salt (page 191)

½ tsp coarsely ground pepper

1 cup (120 g) shredded cheddar cheese (optional)

DIRECTIONS

Preheat the oven to 350°F (177°C). Grease a 15 x 10-inch (38 x 25-cm) sheet pan, then line it with parchment paper.

Add the eggs to a medium bowl. Beat the eggs until they are a pale yellow color. Add the milk, onion, garlic powder, Seasoned Salt and pepper to the eggs and mix well. Stir in the cheese if desired.

Pour the egg mixture into the sheet pan.

Bake the eggs for 20 minutes, or until the eggs are cooked through and starting to separate from the edges of the pan.

Remove the eggs from the oven. Let the eggs sit for 3 to 5 minutes. Use a knife or pizza cutter to cut the eggs into squares.

STORING AND REHEATING

Store the eggs in a sealed container in the refrigerator for up to 3 days.

To freeze, place the slices of egg between layers of parchment paper to keep them from sticking. Store them in a sealed container in the freezer for up to 1 month. Thaw frozen eggs in the refrigerator overnight.

To reheat a thawed square of sheet pan eggs, unwrap it, place it on a microwave-safe plate and microwave on high for 20 seconds.

PUMPKIN-CHAI
EGG PUFFS

This recipe is for everyone who sneaks a piece of pumpkin pie the day after Thanksgiving. Now you can enjoy the flavors of pumpkin pie for breakfast year-round. And if you want to indulge, add a dollop of whipped cream to your egg puff.

INGREDIENTS

6 large eggs

¾ cup (135 g) pureed pumpkin

3 tbsp (27 g) brown sugar

1½ tbsp (15 g) cornstarch

¾ tsp baking powder

1 tbsp (9 g) Chai Spice Mix (page 189)

2 tbsp (30 g) powdered sugar

DIRECTIONS

Grease 6 (4-ounce [180-ml]) ramekins. Preheat the oven to 400°F (204°C).

In a large bowl, combine the eggs, pumpkin, brown sugar, cornstarch, baking powder and Chai Spice Mix. Use a whisk to thoroughly combine the ingredients.

Divide the mixture between the ramekins.

Place the ramekins on a large baking sheet and bake for about 15 minutes, or until the eggs are puffed up, their tops are golden and a toothpick inserted in the centers comes out clean.

Use a flour sifter to sprinkle powdered sugar over the egg puffs.

The egg puffs can be served warm or cool.

STORING AND REHEATING

Cover the egg puffs and store them in the refrigerator for up to 3 days.

To freeze, wrap each egg puff individually and freeze for up to 1 month.

To reheat a thawed egg puff, unwrap it, place it on a microwave-safe plate and microwave on high for 20 to 30 seconds.

To reheat a frozen egg puff, unwrap it, place it on a microwave-safe plate and microwave at 50 percent power for 2 minutes.

**Makes 12**

CAPRESE EGG CUPS

This is a party in a cup. This has the flavors of a caprese appetizer baked into an egg cup. Drizzle the balsamic reduction over the top and the combination of sweet and savory will make you feel like you are indulging in a special treat.

BALSAMIC REDUCTION

1 cup (240 ml) balsamic vinegar

¼ cup (60 ml) honey

EGG CUPS

12 large eggs

¼ tsp Seasoned Salt (page 191)

Dash of coarsely ground pepper

¾ cup (130 g) shredded mozzarella cheese

14 fresh basil leaves, thinly sliced, divided

24 cherry tomatoes, halved

DIRECTIONS

To make the balsamic reduction, add the vinegar and honey to a small pot over medium heat and stir to mix well. Cook until the mixture reaches a boil. Reduce the heat to low and simmer until the mixture has been reduced to about ⅓ cup (80 ml), approximately 30 minutes.

To make the egg cups, preheat the oven to 400°F (204°C). Grease 12 muffin cups.

Add the eggs to a medium bowl and beat with a fork or an egg beater. Add the Seasoned Salt, pepper, mozzarella and most of the basil leaves (reserving some for the tops of the muffins), and stir well.

Divide the egg mixture between the muffin cups. Add 4 cherry tomato halves per muffin cup. Sprinkle the remaining basil over the tops of the muffin cups. Bake for 15 minutes, or until the eggs are cooked through.

To serve, place a Caprese Egg Cup on a plate and drizzle it with the balsamic reduction.

STORING AND REHEATING

Store the Caprese Egg Cups in a sealed container in the refrigerator for up to 3 days.

To freeze, wrap each egg cup individually and freeze for up to 1 month.

To reheat a thawed egg cup, unwrap it, place it on a microwave-safe plate and microwave on high for 20 to 30 seconds.

It is best to thaw an egg cup in the refrigerator overnight, but if you need to reheat a frozen egg cup, unwrap it, place it on a microwave-safe plate and microwave at 50 percent power for 2 minutes.

PIZZA BREAKFAST CUPS

My youngest son is my pickiest eater, but I know that I can get him to eat anything with "pizza" in the name, so these show up on our menu fairly frequently. There is pizza sauce in the topping, but you can serve extra sauce on the side for dipping if you wish.

HASH BROWN CUPS

3 cups (560 g) hash browns, thawed and squeezed of excess moisture

1 tbsp (9 g) Italian Seasoning Mix (page 191)

1 cup (120 g) shredded cheddar cheese

SCRAMBLED EGGS

18 large eggs

4 tsp (12 g) Italian Seasoning Mix (page 191)

1 tsp garlic powder

18 cherry tomatoes, quartered

5 oz (140 g) pepperoni slices, cut into small pieces

½ cup (68 g) diced onion

¼ cup (43 g) diced green bell pepper

TOPPING

1 cup (120 g) Pizza Sauce (page 195)

1 cup (120 g) shredded cheddar cheese

1 cup (130 g) shredded mozzarella cheese

1 green onion, thinly sliced (optional)

DIRECTIONS

To make the hash brown cups, preheat the oven to 400°F (204°C). Grease 24 muffin cups.

In a medium bowl, mix the hash browns and the Italian Seasoning Mix until the hashbrowns are coated. Stir in the cheddar. Divide the hash brown mixture between the 24 muffin cups. Bake for 15 minutes. Remove the muffin cups from the oven and set aside. Do not turn off the oven.

Add the eggs to a medium bowl and use a fork or egg beater to scramble them. Stir in the Italian Seasoning Mix and garlic powder. Stir the cherry tomatoes, pepperoni, onion and bell pepper into the eggs.

Divide the egg mixture between the hash brown cups. Bake for 15 minutes, or until the egg is cooked through. Top with the Pizza Sauce, cheddar, mozzarella and green onion. Bake for 3 to 5 more minutes, or until the cheese melts.

STORING AND REHEATING

Cover the egg cups and store them in the refrigerator for up to 3 days.

To freeze, wrap each egg cup individually and freeze for up to 1 month.

To reheat a thawed egg cup, unwrap it, place it on a microwave-safe plate and microwave on high for 30 to 45 seconds.

To reheat a frozen egg cup, unwrap it, place it on a microwave-safe plate and microwave at 100 percent power for 60 to 90 seconds.

Makes 12

HAM AND BROCCOLI MINI QUICHE WITH HASH BROWN CRUST

I like to make my mini quiches with a hash brown crust because it makes quiche a sturdier to-go breakfast dish. Perfect for those mornings when you don't have time to sit down and eat.

HASH BROWN CRUST

2½ cups (450 g) hash browns, thawed and squeezed of excess moisture

1 tsp onion powder

1 tsp garlic powder

½ tsp Seasoned Salt (page 191)

¼ tsp coarsely ground pepper

FILLING

6 large eggs

1 cup (240 ml) milk

½ tsp garlic powder

¼ tsp Seasoned Salt (page 191)

¼ tsp coarsely ground pepper

1 cup (230 g) diced ham

1 cup (230 g) finely chopped broccoli

1 cup (120 g) shredded cheddar cheese

2 green onions, thinly sliced

DIRECTIONS

To make the hash brown crust, preheat the oven to 400°F (204°C). Grease 12 muffin cups.

In a medium bowl, mix the hash browns with the onion powder, garlic powder, Seasoned Salt and pepper. Press the hash browns into the muffin cups. Bake for 12 minutes, or until the hash browns begin to brown. Remove the hash browns from the oven and set aside. Do not turn off the oven.

To make the filling, add the eggs to a medium bowl. Use a fork or egg beater and beat them until they are a pale yellow color. Add the milk, garlic powder, Seasoned Salt and pepper. Use a fork or whisk to mix well. Add the ham, broccoli, cheddar and green onions to the eggs. Stir well to combine. Divide the quiche filling between the hash brown cups. Bake for 15 minutes, or until the mini quiches are cooked through.

STORING AND REHEATING

Cover the mini quiches and store in the refrigerator for up to 3 days.

To freeze, wrap each mini quiche individually and freeze for up to a month.

To reheat a thawed mini quiche, unwrap it, place it on a microwave-safe plate and microwave on high for 30 to 45 seconds.

To reheat a frozen mini quiche, unwrap it, place it on a microwave-safe plate and microwave at 50 percent power for 2 minutes.

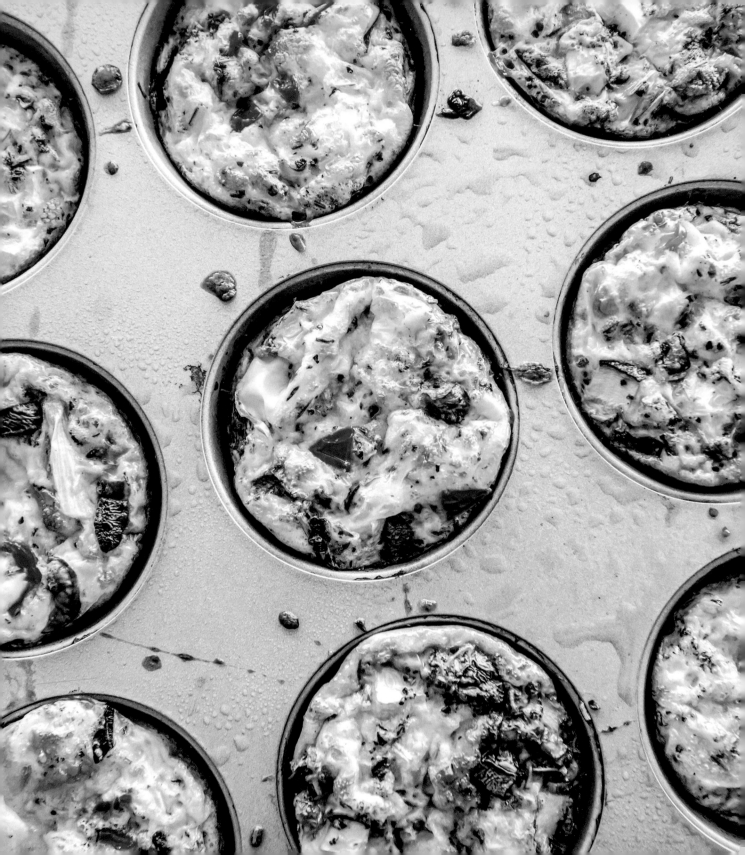

ITALIAN VEGETABLE
MINI FRITTATAS

It is easier to make mini frittatas in a muffin pan than it is to make a traditional frittata. And they turn out just as delicious! Some people like their eggs with ketchup, but my kids like these Italian frittatas dipped in homemade Spaghetti Sauce (page 195).

INGREDIENTS

1 cup (75 g) diced zucchini

12 cherry tomatoes, cut into eighths

⅓ cup (25 g) diced mushrooms

8 large eggs

¼ cup (34 g) diced onion

¼ tsp garlic powder

2 tsp (6 g) Italian Seasoning Mix (page 191)

Dash of coarsely ground pepper

½ cup (65 g) shredded mozzarella cheese

DIRECTIONS

Preheat the oven to 350°F (177°C) and grease a muffin pan.

Divide the zucchini, tomatoes and mushrooms between the muffin cups.

Add the eggs to a medium bowl. Beat the eggs until they are a pale yellow color. Add the onion, garlic powder, Italian Seasoning Mix and pepper to the eggs and mix well.

Divide the egg mixture between the muffin cups. Sprinkle the mozzarella over the tops of the eggs.

Bake for 20 minutes, or until the mini frittatas have set.

Place the muffin pan on a wire rack and allow the mini frittatas to sit for 5 minutes. Run a knife around the outside of each frittata, then lift it out of the muffin cup.

STORING AND REHEATING

Store the mini frittatas in a sealed container in the refrigerator for up to 3 days.

To freeze, wrap each frittata individually and freeze for up to 1 month.

To reheat a thawed frittata, unwrap it, place it on a microwave-safe plate and microwave on high for 20 to 30 seconds.

It is best to thaw a frittata in the refrigerator overnight, but if you need to reheat a frozen frittata, unwrap it, place it on a microwave-safe plate and microwave at 50 percent power for 2 minutes.

CHIPOTLE EGG MUFFIN SANDWICHES

The Chipotle Seasoning Mix and Monterey Jack cheese set this egg muffin sandwich apart from traditional breakfast sandwiches.

Both the eggs and the sausage need to be cooked in the oven. If you time it right by putting the eggs in first and the sausage about ten minutes later, everything will come together at the exact same time.

EGGS

16 large eggs

½ cup (68 g) diced onion

1 cup (170 g) diced green bell pepper

1½ cups (242 g) canned diced tomatoes, drained

3 tbsp (23 g) Chipotle Seasoning Mix (page 192)

SAUSAGE

2 lb (900 g) ground turkey

2 tbsp (30 ml) chicken or vegetable broth

2 tbsp (15 g) Chipotle Seasoning Mix (page 192)

SANDWICHES

12 English muffins or firm rolls

12 slices Monterey Jack cheese

DIRECTIONS

To make the eggs, preheat the oven to 350°F (177°C). Grease 2 (15 x 10-inch [38 x 25-cm]) rimmed baking sheets, then line them with parchment paper.

Add the eggs to a medium bowl. Beat the eggs until they are a pale yellow color. Add the onion, bell pepper, diced tomatoes and Chipotle Seasoning Mix to the eggs. Mix well.

Pour the egg mixture into one of the baking sheets. Bake the eggs for 30 minutes, or until the eggs are cooked through and starting to separate from the edges of the baking sheet. Let the eggs sit for a couple minutes. Then use a knife or pizza cutter to cut the eggs into 12 squares.

While the eggs are cooking, make the sausage by combining the ground turkey, broth and Chipotle Seasoning Mix in a medium bowl.

Spread the turkey mixture out evenly on the other baking sheet so that it touches all of the sides. Bake for 20 minutes. Remove the sausage from the oven and let it sit for a few minutes. Brush off the excess oil with a pastry brush or blot it with a paper towel. Use a knife or pizza cutter to cut the sausage into 12 squares.

To build the breakfast sandwiches, slice the English muffins in half. Place one slice of Monterey Jack, one square of sausage and one square of egg on the bottom of the muffin. Place the top of the muffin on top of the egg.

STORING AND REHEATING

Allow the breakfast sandwiches to cool before storing them. Place them in an airtight container and store in the refrigerator for up to 3 days.

To freeze, wrap each breakfast sandwich individually and freeze for up to 1 month.

To reheat a thawed breakfast sandwich, unwrap it, place it on a microwave-safe plate and microwave on high for 30 to 45 seconds.

To reheat a frozen breakfast sandwich, unwrap it, place it on a microwave-safe plate and microwave at 50 percent power for 3 minutes.

Makes
12

CAJUN EGG CROISSANT SANDWICHES

There are a couple of steps involved in creating these croissant breakfast sandwiches, but they really aren't that hard to make. And boy, are they worth the effort!

EGGS

16 large eggs

½ cup (68 g) diced red onion

½ cup (85 g) diced red bell pepper

1½ cups (100 g) thinly sliced asparagus

2 tbsp (4 g) Cajun Seasoning Mix (page 190)

SAUSAGE

2 lb (950 g) ground pork

2 tbsp (30 ml) chicken or vegetable broth

2 tbsp (4 g) Cajun Seasoning Mix (page 190)

SANDWICHES

12 croissants

12 slices medium cheddar cheese

DIRECTIONS

To make the eggs, preheat the oven to 350°F (177°C). Grease 2 (15 x 10-inch [38 x 25-cm]) rimmed baking sheets, then line them with parchment paper.

Add the eggs to a medium bowl. Beat the eggs until they are a pale yellow color. Add the onion, bell pepper, asparagus and Cajun Seasoning Mix to the eggs. Mix well.

Pour the egg mixture into one of the baking sheets. Bake the eggs for 30 minutes, or until the eggs are cooked through and starting to separate from the edges of the pan. Remove the baking sheet from the oven and let the eggs sit for a couple minutes. Use a knife or pizza cutter to cut the eggs into 12 squares.

While the eggs are cooking, make the sausage by combining the pork, broth and Cajun Seasoning Mix in a medium bowl.

Spread the pork mixture out evenly on the other baking sheet so that it touches all of the sides. Bake for 20 minutes. Remove the sausage from the oven and let it sit for a few minutes. Brush off the excess oil with a pastry brush or blot it with a paper towel. Then use a knife or pizza cutter to cut the sausage into 12 squares.

To build the breakfast sandwiches, slice the croissants in half. Place one slice of cheddar, one square of sausage and one square of egg on the bottom of the croissant. Place the top of the croissant on top of the egg.

STORING AND REHEATING

Allow the breakfast sandwiches to cool before storing them. Place them in an airtight container and store in the refrigerator for up to 3 days.

To freeze, wrap each breakfast sandwich individually and freeze for up to 1 month.

To reheat a thawed breakfast sandwich, unwrap it, place it on a microwave-safe plate and microwave on high for 30 to 45 seconds.

To reheat a frozen breakfast sandwich, unwrap it, place it on a microwave-safe plate and microwave at 50 percent power for 3 minutes.

GREEK STEAK AND
EGGS PITA POCKETS

What could be better in a breakfast pita pocket than Greek steak and eggs? The steak and eggs are infused with the flavor of the herbs. I love any dish that gets my family to voluntarily consume vegetables at breakfast!

STEAK

1 tbsp (15 ml) olive oil

1 tbsp (15 ml) red wine vinegar

1¼ lb (563 g) steak, cut into bite-size pieces

¼ cup (34 g) diced red onion

¼ cup (34 g) diced celery

¼ tsp dried oregano

¼ tsp dried basil

EGGS

10 large eggs

¼ cup (45 g) sliced black olives

½ cup (38 g) diced mushrooms

⅔ cup (108 g) diced fresh tomatoes

½ tsp dried oregano

½ tsp dried basil

⅛ tsp Seasoned Salt (page 191)

⅛ tsp coarsely ground pepper

PITA POCKETS

4 pitas, cut in half

4 oz (112 g) crumbled feta cheese

DIRECTIONS

To make the steak, heat the oil and vinegar in a large skillet over medium-high heat. Add the steak, onion and celery. Cook until the steak is browned on all sides, approximately 7 minutes. Add the oregano and basil and toss to coat the steak in the herbs. Reduce the heat to medium-low and cook for 4 to 5 minutes, or until the steak is cooked through and the juices run clear. Remove the steak from the skillet and use it to cook the eggs.

To make the eggs, beat the eggs in a large bowl until they are a pale yellow color. Stir in the olives, mushrooms, tomatoes, oregano, basil, Seasoned Salt and pepper.

Pour the egg mixture into the skillet and cook over medium-low heat, without stirring, for 1 to 2 minutes, until the eggs start to set on the bottom and along the edges of the skillet. Using a spatula, gently lift and fold the egg mixture, so that the uncooked mixture runs underneath and onto the bottom of the skillet (you will have to repeat this step several times). Cook for 2 to 3 minutes, or until the eggs are thoroughly cooked.

To assemble the pita pockets, add ½ cup (115 g) scrambled eggs to a pita. Then add ¼ cup (58 g) steak and sprinkle the feta over the pita pocket.

STORING AND REHEATING

Allow the pita pockets to cool before storing. Place them in an airtight container and store them in the refrigerator for up to 3 days.

To freeze, wrap each pita pocket individually and freeze for up to 1 month.

To reheat a thawed pita pocket, unwrap it, place it on a microwave-safe plate and microwave on high for 30 to 45 seconds.

To reheat a frozen pita pocket, unwrap it, place it on a microwave-safe plate and microwave at 50 percent power for 3 minutes.

CHIMICHURRI STEAK
BREAKFAST BURRITO

We love grilled steak with Chimichurri Sauce in the summer. This breakfast burrito allows us to enjoy the flavors year-round. When you make the burritos, you will have some of the Chimichurri Sauce leftover. Save it for dipping the burritos in.

CHIMICHURRI SAUCE

1 cup (40 g) loosely packed fresh parsley leaves

1 cup (40 g) loosely packed fresh cilantro leaves

¼ cup (34 g) chopped onion

2 tbsp (30 ml) olive oil

1 tbsp (15 ml) distilled white vinegar

1 tbsp (15 ml) lime juice

1 tbsp (3 g) fresh basil or 1 tsp dried basil

1 tbsp (3 g) fresh oregano or 1 tsp dried oregano

1 tbsp (3 g) fresh thyme or 1 tsp dried thyme

2 tsp (10 ml) honey

4 cloves garlic

¼ tsp cayenne

Pinch of Seasoned Salt (page 191)

BURRITOS

1 tbsp (15 ml) olive oil

1 lb (450 g) steak, cut into bite-size pieces

8 large eggs

¼ cup (60 ml) milk

½ cup (85 g) diced green bell pepper

½ cup (68 g) diced red onion

¼ tsp garlic powder

Dash of coarsely ground pepper

6 (10-inch [25-cm]) tortillas

¾ cup (98 g) shredded Monterey Jack cheese

DIRECTIONS

To make the chimichurri sauce, add the parsley, cilantro, onion, oil, vinegar, lime juice, basil, oregano, thyme, honey, garlic, cayenne and Seasoned Salt to a food processor or blender and puree until smooth.

To make the burritos, heat the oil in a large skillet over medium-high heat. Add the steak and cook until it is browned on all sides, approximately 5 minutes. Reduce the heat to medium-low and cook for 4 to 5 minutes, or until the steak is cooked through and the juices run clear. Remove the steak from the skillet and use it to cook the eggs.

In a large bowl, beat the eggs until they are a pale yellow color. Stir in the milk, bell pepper, onion, garlic powder and pepper.

Pour the egg mixture into the skillet and cook over medium-low heat, without stirring, for 1 to 2 minutes, until the eggs start to set on the bottom and around the edges of the skillet. Using a spatula, gently lift and fold the egg mixture, so that the uncooked mixture runs underneath and onto the bottom of the skillet (you will have to repeat this step several times). Cook for 2 to 3 minutes, or until the eggs are thoroughly cooked.

To build the breakfast burritos, divide the scrambled eggs between the tortillas, placing them just slightly off-center. Add the steak. Spoon 1 to 2 tablespoons (15 to 30 ml) of the Chimichurri Sauce over the steak. Sprinkle the Monterey Jack over the steak and eggs. Fold the bottom and top of the tortillas toward the middle. Fold the short side of the tortillas over and then keep rolling until they are closed.

STORING AND REHEATING

Allow the burritos to cool before storing. Place them in an airtight container and store them in the refrigerator for up to 3 days.

To freeze, wrap each burrito individually and freeze for up to 1 month.

To reheat a thawed burrito, unwrap it, place it on a microwave-safe plate and microwave on high for 30 to 45 seconds.

To reheat a frozen burrito, unwrap it, place it on a microwave-safe plate and microwave at 50 percent power for 3 minutes.

Chapter 2

QUICK BREAKFAST BREADS

Waffles, pancakes, muffins and biscuits are perfect for making in large batches on the weekend and freezing to use for breakfasts throughout the week. Breakfast breads can be stored in the freezer for up to 3 months, so go ahead and make a double batch of your favorite waffles.

PEANUT BUTTER CHOCOLATE CHIP BLENDER PANCAKES

This is a quick and easy pancake recipe. And since it includes peanut butter and chocolate chips, it is a hit with the whole family. These do not need any syrup, but we may be guilty of topping them with a little chocolate syrup (and even whipped cream on occasion).

INGREDIENTS

1⅓ cups (173 g) finely ground oat flour

1 cup (240 ml) milk

¼ cup (45 g) smooth peanut butter

1 large egg

2 tbsp (18 g) brown sugar

2 tsp (8 g) baking powder

½ tsp vanilla extract

½ cup (90 g) mini chocolate chips

½ cup (120 ml) chocolate syrup (optional)

Whipped cream (optional)

DIRECTIONS

Add the flour, milk, peanut butter, egg, brown sugar, baking powder and vanilla to a blender. Blend until smooth. Stir the chocolate chips into the batter.

Lightly oil and heat a large skillet over medium heat.

Pour about ¼ cup (60 ml) of batter for each pancake into the skillet. Cook for 3 to 5 minutes, until the tops are covered with bubbles and the edges look cooked. Flip the pancakes and cook for 2 to 3 minutes, until they are golden brown.

Top with chocolate syrup and whipped cream if you'd like.

STORING AND REHEATING

Once the pancakes are cool, store them in an airtight container or sealable freezer bag. Place parchment paper between the pancakes to prevent them from freezing together. Freeze for up to 3 months.

Reheat a frozen pancake by placing it in a microwave-safe dish. Microwave on high for 1 minute or until the pancake is heated through.

You can also reheat the frozen pancakes in the oven. Place them in a single layer on a baking sheet and cover them with foil. Bake at 375°F (191°C) for 8 to 10 minutes, or until the pancakes are heated through.

LEMON CHIA SEED WAFFLES

If you like lemon poppy seed bread, you will love these waffles. They have a bright, lemony flavor as well as chia seeds, which have more protein than poppy seeds. These waffles pair well with Blueberry Syrup (page 198).

INGREDIENTS

1½ cups (188 g) all-purpose flour

¼ cup (48 g) sugar

2 tsp (8 g) baking soda

¼ tsp salt

2 large eggs

1 cup + 2 tbsp (270 ml) milk

6 tbsp (90 ml) lemon juice

Zest of 2 lemons

¼ cup (60 ml) mild-tasting oil, plus more for cooking

½ cup (123 g) lemon yogurt

2 tbsp (16 g) chia seeds

DIRECTIONS

Preheat the waffle iron.

In a small bowl, combine the flour, sugar, baking soda and salt.

Add the eggs to a medium bowl. Beat with a fork or an egg beater. Add the milk, lemon juice, lemon zest, oil and yogurt to the eggs. Stir well to thoroughly combine. Stir the flour mixture into the egg mixture until fully incorporated. Stir the chia seeds into the batter.

Lightly coat the waffle iron with oil. Add the batter to the waffle iron in the amount recommended by its manufacturer. When the light on the waffle maker indicates that the waffles are done, check to make sure they are golden brown. If not, close the lid and cook for an additional minute. Repeat this process until you have cooked all of the batter.

STORING AND REHEATING

Once the waffles are cool, store them in an airtight container or sealable freezer bag. Freeze for up to 3 months.

Reheat a frozen waffle by placing it in the toaster. You may have to toast it for 2 cycles to heat it all the way through.

Makes 10

JALAPEÑO CORN BREAD WAFFLES

These waffles meld the flavors of corn bread with jalapeño poppers. Instead of butter, spread cream cheese on these waffles, and instead of syrup, employ salsa as your topping.

INGREDIENTS

1 cup (125 g) all-purpose flour

¾ cup (128 g) cornmeal

1 tbsp (12 g) sugar

2 tsp (8 g) baking soda

¼ tsp Seasoned Salt (page 191)

2 large eggs

2 cups (480 ml) milk

½ cup (62 g) ricotta cheese, softened

¼ cup (60 ml) olive oil, plus more for cooking

2 medium jalapeño peppers, deseeded and diced

2 green onions, thinly sliced

½ cup (60 g) shredded cheddar cheese

½ cup (65 g) shredded Monterey Jack cheese

DIRECTIONS

Preheat the waffle iron.

Add the flour, cornmeal, sugar, baking soda and Seasoned Salt to a small bowl. Stir to combine.

Add the eggs to a medium bowl. Beat the eggs with a fork or egg beater. Add the milk, ricotta and oil to the eggs. Stir well to combine. Add the flour mixture to the egg mixture and stir until fully incorporated. Add the jalapeños, green onions, cheddar and Monterey Jack to the batter. Stir to combine.

Lightly coat the waffle iron with oil. Add the batter to the waffle iron in the amount recommended by its manufacturer. When the light on the waffle maker indicates that the waffles are done, check to make sure they are golden brown. If not, close the lid and cook for an additional minute. Repeat this process until you have cooked all of the batter.

STORING AND REHEATING

Once the waffles are cool, store them in an airtight container or sealable freezer bag. Freeze for up to 3 months.

Reheat a frozen waffle by placing it in the toaster. You may have to toast it for 2 cycles to heat it all the way through.

GARLIC AND ROSEMARY SWEET POTATO PANCAKES

Sometimes it is okay to let sweet potatoes be potatoes and pair them with savory spices. Instead of covering these in syrup, we like to dip these pancakes in bread-dipping oil.

INGREDIENTS

1¼ cups (156 g) all-purpose flour

1 tbsp (12 g) baking powder

2 tsp (2 g) crushed rosemary

1 tsp garlic powder

¼ tsp Seasoned Salt (page 191)

4 large eggs

1 cup (240 ml) milk

¼ cup (60 ml) olive oil

1½ cups (270 g) pureed sweet potato

2 green onions, thinly sliced

DIRECTIONS

In a small bowl, combine the flour, baking powder, rosemary, garlic powder and Seasoned Salt.

Add the eggs to a medium bowl and beat with a fork or egg beater. Add the milk, oil and sweet potato to the eggs. Mix well. Add the flour mixture to the egg mixture and stir until fully incorporated. Stir the green onions into the batter.

Lightly oil and heat a large skillet over medium heat.

Pour about ¼ cup (60 ml) of batter for each pancake into the skillet. Cook for 3 to 5 minutes, until the tops are covered with bubbles and the edges look cooked. Flip the pancakes and cook for 2 to 3 minutes, until they are golden brown.

STORING AND REHEATING

Once the pancakes are cool, store them in an airtight container or sealable freezer bag. Place parchment paper between the pancakes to prevent them from freezing together. Freeze for up to 3 months.

Reheat a frozen pancake by placing it in a microwave-safe dish. Microwave on high for 1 minute or until the pancake is heated through.

You can also reheat the frozen pancakes in the oven. Place them in a single layer on a baking sheet and cover them with foil. Bake at 375°F (191°C) for 8 to 10 minutes, or until the pancakes are heated through.

CHICKEN-FAJITA STUFFED FRENCH TOAST

This is a hearty and flavorful way to start the day. Because it is almost a sandwich, you can eat it on the run; but if you have time to sit down, savor it while dipping it in salsa.

FILLING

1 tbsp (15 ml) olive oil

1 lb (450 g) boneless, skinless chicken breast or thigh, cut into thin strips

1 medium green bell pepper, cut into ¼-inch (6-mm) thick strips

1 medium red bell pepper, cut into ¼-inch (6-mm) thick strips

½ cup (65 g) thinly sliced red onion

1 tbsp (9 g) Taco Seasoning Mix (page 190)

FRENCH TOAST

4 large eggs

½ cup (120 ml) milk

1 tbsp (9 g) Taco Seasoning Mix (page 190)

1 tbsp (15 ml) olive oil

24 slices sandwich bread

12 slices medium cheddar cheese

12 slices Monterey Jack cheese

DIRECTIONS

To make the filling, heat the oil in a large skillet over medium heat. Add the chicken and cook for 4 to 5 minutes, or until the chicken is browned. Add the green bell pepper, red bell pepper, onion and Taco Seasoning Mix. Toss to coat the chicken and vegetables. Cook for approximately 5 minutes, until the chicken is cooked through.

To make the French toast, add the eggs, milk and Taco Seasoning Mix to a shallow dish. Use a whisk or fork to blend the ingredients.

Heat the oil in a large skillet over medium heat.

Add 2 slices of bread to the egg mixture. Soak only one side of the bread. Do not flip the slices over.

Place the bread, soaked-side down, in the skillet. Top one piece of bread with a slice of cheddar and top the other piece with a slice of Monterey Jack. Add the filling to the slice with the cheddar. Once the Monterey Jack has melted and the bread has browned, flip it cheese-side down on top of the filling. Remove the Chicken-Fajita Stuffed French Toast from the skillet.

Repeat this process with the remainder of the ingredients.

STORING AND REHEATING

Once the French toast is cool, place it in an airtight container in the refrigerator for up to 3 days.

To freeze, place parchment paper or wax paper between the French toast, then place it in a sealable freezer bag. You can freeze French toast for up to 1 month.

To reheat, preheat the oven to 400°F (204°C). Place the French toast on a lightly greased baking sheet. Cook for 5 to 6 minutes on each side. Take a core sample to ensure it is heated through.

You can also reheat French toast in a microwave on high for 30 to 60 seconds, but it won't be as crisp.

PEACHES AND CREAM STUFFED FRENCH TOAST

These taste like you are eating a peach hand pie instead of French toast. Instead of maple syrup, drizzle Apple Cinnamon Syrup (page 199) over this delicious breakfast.

FILLING

6 oz (170 g) cream cheese, softened

½ cup (65 g) powdered sugar

1 tbsp (15 ml) vanilla extract

1½ tsp (4 g) ground cinnamon, divided

1½ tsp (4 g) grated fresh ginger, divided

1¾ cups (264 g) canned diced peaches, drained

FRENCH TOAST

4 large eggs

½ cup (120 ml) milk

1 tsp ground cinnamon

1 tsp grated fresh ginger

1 tbsp (15 g) butter

24 slices sandwich bread

¼ cup (32 g) powdered sugar (optional)

Maple syrup (optional)

DIRECTIONS

To make the filling, combine the cream cheese, powdered sugar, vanilla, 1 teaspoon of the cinnamon and 1 teaspoon of the ginger in a small bowl.

In a medium bowl, combine the peaches with the remaining ½ teaspoon of cinnamon and the remaining ½ teaspoon of ginger until the peaches are evenly coated.

To make the French toast, add the eggs, milk, cinnamon and ginger to a shallow dish. Use a whisk or fork to blend the ingredients.

Heat the butter in a large skillet over medium heat.

Add 2 slices of bread to the egg mixture. Soak only one side of the bread. Do not flip the slices over.

Place the bread, soaked-side down, in the skillet. Spread a thin layer of the cream cheese mixture on top of the bread. Add 1 tablespoon (9 g) of peaches to the center of one of the slices of bread. Flip the other piece of french toast, cream cheese–side down, on top of the peaches. Cook for 3 to 5 minutes, until the bottom slice of bread is brown. Flip the French toast and cook for 3 to 5 minutes, until the other side is brown. Remove the French toast from the skillet.

Repeat this process with the remainder of the ingredients.

Sprinkle with powdered sugar and/or top with syrup.

STORING AND REHEATING

Once the French toast is cool, place it in an airtight container in the refrigerator for up to 3 days.

To freeze, place parchment paper or wax paper between the French toast, then place it in a sealable freezer bag. You can freeze French toast for up to 1 month.

To reheat, preheat the oven to 400°F (204°C). Place the French toast on a lightly greased baking sheet. Cook for 5 to 6 minutes on each side. Take a core sample to ensure it is heated through.

You can also reheat French toast in a microwave on high for 30 to 60 seconds, but it won't be as crisp.

HAM AND CHEESE RANCH DROP BISCUITS

For those days when you don't have time to sit down to breakfast, these savory drop biscuits make the perfect on-the-go breakfast!

INGREDIENTS

1 cup (240 ml) milk

1 tbsp (15 ml) lemon juice

1½ cups (188 g) all-purpose flour

2½ tsp (10 g) baking powder

2 tsp (6 g) onion powder

2 tsp (6 g) garlic powder

2 tsp (2 g) dried parsley

½ tsp dried basil

¼ tsp ground mustard

¼ tsp dried dill

⅛ tsp Seasoned Salt (page 191)

⅛ tsp coarsely ground pepper

6 tbsp (84 g) cold butter

1 cup (230 g) diced ham

1 cup (120 g) shredded medium cheddar cheese

1 cup (240 g) finely chopped broccoli

DIRECTIONS

Preheat the oven to 350°F (177°C). Grease 2 medium baking sheets.

Add the milk and lemon juice to a small bowl. Allow the mixture to sit for 5 minutes.

Add the flour, baking powder, onion powder, garlic powder, parsley, basil, ground mustard, dill, Seasoned Salt and pepper to a large bowl. Cut the butter into the flour with a knife or pastry blender until the mixture resembles coarse crumbs. Slowly add the milk, stirring it into the flour until it is fully incorporated. Add the ham, cheese and broccoli to the batter, stirring until they are completely mixed in.

Drop the batter by heaping spoonfuls onto the baking sheets. Bake for 18 to 22 minutes, or until the tops are lightly browned.

STORING AND REHEATING

Cool the biscuits completely before storing. Store the biscuits in a single layer in an airtight container or sealable bag. You can store the biscuits in the container in the refrigerator for up to 3 days or in the freezer for up to 3 months.

Allow frozen biscuits to thaw in the refrigerator. You can warm them individually in the microwave for 20 to 30 seconds on high. You can warm up a batch of biscuits by placing them in a baking dish, covering the dish with foil, and baking them at 350°F (177°C) for 10 to 12 minutes.

HUMMINGBIRD ZUCCHINI MUFFINS

I combined the flavors of hummingbird cake with zucchini bread to make these tasty muffins a bit healthier. Hummingbird cake usually has a cream cheese frosting, so feel free to serve these with cream cheese.

INGREDIENTS

1½ cups (188 g) all-purpose flour

¾ cup (60 g) old-fashioned rolled oats

⅔ cup (96 g) brown sugar

2 tsp (6 g) ground cinnamon

1¼ tsp (5 g) baking soda

¼ tsp salt

3 large eggs

½ cup (123 g) applesauce

¼ cup (60 ml) mild-tasting oil

½ cup (120 ml) water

1 tsp vanilla extract

1½ cups (270 g) diced banana

¾ cup (185 g) crushed pineapple, with liquid

1½ cups (99 g) shredded zucchini

DIRECTIONS

Preheat the oven to 350°F (177°C). Grease 2 muffin pans (or line them with baking cups).

In a large bowl, combine the flour, oats, brown sugar, cinnamon, baking soda and salt.

Add the eggs, applesauce, oil and water to the flour mixture. Stir by hand until the dry ingredients are moist.

Stir in the vanilla, banana, pineapple and zucchini.

Spoon the batter into the muffin cups. Bake the muffins for 20 minutes, or until a toothpick inserted into the center of a muffin comes out clean.

STORING AND REHEATING

Cool the muffins completely before storing. Store the muffins in a single layer in an airtight container or sealable bag. Place a paper towel below the muffins and another paper towel on top of the muffins to absorb any moisture. You can store the muffins in the container on the counter for up to 3 days or in the freezer for up to 3 months.

Allow frozen muffins to thaw on the counter. You can eat the muffins when they reach room temperature or warm them in the microwave for 20 to 30 seconds on high. You can warm up a batch of muffins by placing them in a baking dish, covering the dish with foil and baking them at 350°F (177°C) for 10 to 12 minutes.

Makes 12

CHOCOLATE HAZELNUT MUFFINS

Hazelnut meal replaces some of the flour in this recipe. When you use a nut meal or nut flour in a recipe, you can reduce the amount of oil you use, because nuts naturally contain oil that is released in the baking process.

INGREDIENTS

⅓ cup (37 g) unsweetened cocoa powder

1 cup (240 ml) hot water

1¼ cups (156 g) all-purpose flour

¼ cup (24 g) hazelnut meal

⅔ cup (128 g) sugar

1 tsp baking soda

¼ tsp salt

¼ cup (60 ml) mild-tasting oil

2 large eggs

1 tsp vanilla extract

DIRECTIONS

Preheat the oven to 350°F (177°C). Grease a muffin pan (or line it with baking cups).

In a small bowl, combine the cocoa powder and water. Set aside.

In a large bowl, combine the flour, hazelnut meal, sugar, baking soda and salt.

Add the oil, eggs and vanilla to the cocoa mixture and stir well to combine. Add the cocoa powder mixture to the flour mixture and stir until just combined.

Spoon the batter into the muffin cups. Bake for 20 minutes, or until a toothpick inserted into the center of a muffin comes out clean.

STORING AND REHEATING

Cool the muffins completely before storing. Store the muffins in a single layer in an airtight container or sealable bag. Place a paper towel below the muffins and another paper towel on top of the muffins to absorb any moisture. You can store the muffins in the container on the counter for up to 3 days or in the freezer for up to 3 months.

Allow frozen muffins to thaw on the counter. You can eat the muffins when they reach room temperature or warm them in the microwave for 20 to 30 seconds on high. You can warm up a batch of muffins by placing them in a baking dish, covering the dish with foil and baking them at 350°F (177°C) for 10 to 12 minutes.

CHAI-SPICED CARROT CAKE MUFFINS

I use a quadruple-strength cup of chai tea to add extra flavor to these carrot cake muffins. For a decadent treat, serve the muffins with cream cheese.

INGREDIENTS

1 cup (240 ml) boiling hot water

4 chai tea bags

1 cup (125 g) all-purpose flour

⅔ cup (53 g) old-fashioned rolled oats

½ cup (72 g) brown sugar

1 tsp Chai Spice Mix (page 189)

¾ tsp baking soda

¼ tsp salt

¼ cup (60 ml) mild-tasting oil

1 tsp vanilla extract

1 large egg

1 cup (341 g) shredded carrots

½ cup (58 g) chopped walnuts (optional)

DIRECTIONS

Preheat the oven to 350°F (177°C). Grease a muffin pan (or line it with baking cups).

In a small pot over high heat, bring the water to a boil. Remove the pot from the heat, add the tea bags to the water and let them steep for 5 minutes. Squeeze the excess liquid from the tea bags, then measure the amount of tea. Add enough water to bring it back to 1 cup (240 ml) of liquid.

In a large bowl, combine the flour, oats, brown sugar, Chai Spice Mix, baking soda and salt.

Add the tea, oil, vanilla and egg to the flour mixture and stir well to combine. Add the carrots and walnuts if desired and stir gently to combine.

Spoon the batter into the muffin cups. Bake for 20 minutes, or until a toothpick inserted into the center of a muffin comes out clean.

STORING AND REHEATING

Cool the muffins completely before storing. Store the muffins in a single layer in an airtight container or sealable bag. Place a paper towel below the muffins and another paper towel on top of the muffins to absorb any moisture. You can store the muffins in the container on the counter for up to 3 days or in the freezer for up to 3 months.

Allow frozen muffins to thaw on the counter. You can eat the muffins when they reach room temperature or warm them in the microwave for 20 to 30 seconds on high. You can warm up a batch of muffins by placing them in a baking dish, covering the dish with foil and baking them at 350°F (177°C) for 10 to 12 minutes.

Makes 18

PUMPKIN QUINOA MUFFINS

Pumpkin muffins are a favorite at my house. I like to use quinoa flour to add a little extra protein without altering the flavor too much.

INGREDIENTS

1½ cups (188 g) all-purpose flour

½ cup (76 g) quinoa flour

1 tbsp (12 g) baking powder

5 tsp (15 g) Pumpkin Pie Spice Mix (page 192)

4 large eggs

1 cup (240 ml) milk

⅓ cup (80 ml) mild-tasting oil

1¾ cups (315 g) pureed pumpkin

½ cup (72 g) brown sugar

DIRECTIONS

Preheat the oven to 350°F (177°C). Grease 18 muffin cups (or line them with baking cups).

In a medium bowl, combine the all-purpose flour, quinoa flour, baking powder and Pumpkin Pie Spice Mix.

In a large bowl, combine the eggs, milk, oil, pumpkin and brown sugar, stirring well.

Add the flour mixture to the pumpkin mixture. Mix everything together until it is just combined.

Spoon the batter into the muffin cups. Bake for 25 minutes, or until a toothpick inserted into the center of a muffin comes out clean.

STORING AND REHEATING

Cool the muffins completely before storing. Store the muffins in a single layer in an airtight container or sealable bag. Place a paper towel below the muffins and another paper towel on top of the muffins to absorb any moisture. You can store the muffins in the container on the counter for up to 3 days or in the freezer for up to 3 months.

Allow frozen muffins to thaw on the counter. You can eat the muffins when they reach room temperature or warm them in the microwave for 20 to 30 seconds on high. You can warm up a batch of muffins by placing them in a baking dish, covering the dish with foil and baking them at 350°F (177°C) for 10 to 12 minutes.

Chapter 3

HOT AND COLD CEREALS THAT SATISFY

Some of us just want cereal for breakfast. You will have success with homemade cereals if you choose a preparation method that fits your schedule. If you have absolutely no time in the morning, then a grab-and-go overnight refrigerator oatmeal might be for you. If you like hot oatmeal, but don't have a lot of time to cook it in the morning, you may enjoy the overnight slow cooker oatmeal recipes; or perhaps it would be easier to grab one of the homemade instant oatmeal packets, pour it into a bowl, add hot water and stir. If you crave sweets in the morning, then make a baked oatmeal ahead of time and reheat it in the microwave. It will be like eating a warm piece of coffee cake—without the guilt. Want cold cereal and milk? Make a triple batch of overnight granola, so you always have some on hand.

STRAWBERRY RHUBARB
BAKED OATMEAL

This Strawberry Rhubarb Baked Oatmeal is tasty enough that you could get away with serving it for dessert. The texture is similiar to coffee cake, which makes it an enjoyable way to eat oats and fruit in the morning.

INGREDIENTS

2 large eggs

2 cups (480 ml) milk

3 tbsp (42 g) butter, melted

⅔ cup (96 g) brown sugar

2 cups (160 g) old-fashioned rolled oats

1 tbsp (12 g) baking powder

2 tsp (6 g) ground cinnamon

¼ tsp salt

2 cups (303 g) diced strawberries

2 cups (340 g) diced rhubarb

⅓ cup (40 g) chopped pecans

DIRECTIONS

Preheat the oven to 325°F (163°C) and grease a 13 x 9-inch (33 x 23-cm) baking dish.

In a large bowl, whisk together the eggs, milk, butter and brown sugar. Add the oats, baking powder, cinnamon and salt and mix until thoroughly combined. Stir the strawberries and rhubarb into the oatmeal.

Pour the oatmeal into the greased baking dish. Sprinkle the chopped pecans over the top. Bake for 40 minutes.

STORING AND REHEATING

You can cover the dish with foil and refrigerate this baked oatmeal for up to 5 days. Reheat individual slices in the microwave on high for 30 to 45 seconds.

Allow the oatmeal to cool off a bit before freezing. You can cut the baked oatmeal up into individual servings, wrap and freeze. Microwave a frozen serving on 50 percent power for 3 minutes, or until it is heated through.

APPLE PIE
BAKED OATMEAL

Not only does this baked oatmeal have apples in it, applesauce is substituted for the oil. It has a rich apple flavor and very little fat. I like to use Fuji apples in this recipe, but you can use any crisp, sweet apple that is in season.

INGREDIENTS

2 large eggs

½ cup (123 g) applesauce

2 cups (480 ml) milk

½ cup (72 g) brown sugar

2 cups (160 g) old-fashioned rolled oats

1 tbsp (12 g) baking powder

2 tsp (6 g) Apple Pie Spice Mix (page 189)

¼ tsp salt

2 medium apples, peeled, cored and diced

DIRECTIONS

Preheat the oven to 325°F (163°C) and grease a 13 x 9-inch (33 x 23-cm) baking dish.

In a large bowl, whisk together the eggs, applesauce, milk and brown sugar. Add the oats, baking powder, Apple Pie Spice Mix and salt and mix until thoroughly combined. Stir the apples into the oat mixture.

Pour the oatmeal into the greased baking dish. Bake for 40 minutes.

STORING AND REHEATING

You can cover the dish with foil and refrigerate this baked oatmeal for up to 5 days. Reheat individual slices in the microwave on high for 30 to 45 seconds.

Allow the oatmeal to cool off a bit before freezing. You can cut the baked oatmeal up into individual servings, wrap and freeze. Microwave a frozen serving on 50 percent power for 3 minutes, or until it is heated through.

Makes 1 packet

OATMEAL PACKETS

Pre-made oatmeal packets are one of the easiest prep-ahead breakfasts ever. Each member of the family can pick their favorite flavor and you can keep a stash of oatmeal packets on hand for super busy mornings.

CINNAMON SPICE OATMEAL

½ cup (40 g) instant oatmeal

1 tbsp (8 g) oat flour

1 tsp flax meal

2 tsp (6 g) brown sugar

2 tsp (5 g) powdered milk

½ tsp ground cinnamon

¼ tsp ground ginger

Pinch of ground nutmeg

CHAI-SPICED APPLE OATMEAL

½ cup (40 g) instant oatmeal

1 tbsp (8 g) oat flour

¼ cup (23 g) dried apple pieces

1 tbsp (7 g) powdered milk

2 tsp (10 g) brown sugar

½ tsp Chai Spice Mix (page 189)

BLUEBERRY-WALNUT OATMEAL

½ cup (40 g) instant oatmeal

1 tbsp (8 g) oat flour

¼ cup (38 g) dried blueberries

2 tbsp (15 g) chopped walnuts

1 tsp flax meal

2 tsp (5 g) powdered milk

2 tsp (10 g) brown sugar

¼ tsp ground nutmeg

DIRECTIONS

Choose the flavor you wish to make. Add all of the ingredients for that variation of oatmeal to a sealable bag or container.

To serve, pour an oatmeal packet into a heat-proof bowl. Bring ¾ cup (180 ml) to 1 cup (240 ml) of water to a boil in a small pot over high heat. Slowly add the boiling water to the oatmeal, stirring until it reaches the desired consistency.

STORING

Label each oatmeal packet with the recipe name and date. Store the oatmeal packets in the pantry for up to 1 month.

OVERNIGHT REFRIGERATOR OATMEAL

Overnight oatmeal was a game changer in our house. It opened up more possibilities than the oatmeal packets. Fresh fruit, nut butters, yogurt and molasses have all found their way into our canning jars of refrigerator oatmeal.

Most people think you have to make these the night before and eat them the next morning. But here is a secret: as long as you aren't making a variation that contains fresh fruit, you can make a week's worth of oatmeal on Sunday night and enjoy it all week long.

If you are tired of oatmeal, you can substitute buckwheat in these overnight refrigerator recipes. It will be firmer and chewier than oatmeal. I enjoy it, but it is a matter of personal taste.

CHOCOLATE PEANUT BUTTER OVERNIGHT OATMEAL

½ cup (40 g) old-fashioned rolled oats

⅔ cup (160 ml) chocolate almond or cashew milk

2 tbsp (23 g) smooth peanut butter

2 tbsp (15 g) hemp protein powder

1 tsp flax meal

PEACHES AND CREAM OVERNIGHT OATMEAL

½ cup (40 g) old-fashioned rolled oats

⅓ cup (80 ml) vanilla almond milk

½ cup (123 g) peach Greek yogurt

1 medium peach, peeled and diced

¼ tsp ground cinnamon

⅛ tsp ground nutmeg

GINGERBREAD OVERNIGHT OATMEAL

½ cup (40 g) old-fashioned rolled oats

⅔ cup (160 ml) vanilla almond milk

2 tbsp (15 g) hemp protein powder

1 tsp flax meal

1 tsp molasses

1 tsp brown sugar

¼ tsp ground cinnamon

¼ tsp ground ginger

Pinch of ground nutmeg

DIRECTIONS

Add the oats to a 16-ounce (480-ml) Mason jar or another lidded container.

Add the milk to the oats and stir well. Add the rest of the ingredients. Stir until thoroughly mixed and seal the container.

Refrigerate the oatmeal overnight or until the liquid is absorbed and the oats are soft, 6 to 8 hours. Serve the oatmeal cold or remove the lid and heat it in the microwave for 1 minute.

STORING

Label each oatmeal packet with the recipe name and date.

The peaches and cream oatmeal can be stored in the refrigerator for 2 to 3 days.

The chocolate peanut butter oatmeal and gingerbread oatmeal can be stored in the refrigerator for up to 5 days.

OVERNIGHT PUMPKIN PIE-SPICED PECAN GRANOLA

Every once in a while, you just want to enjoy a bowl of cereal. This overnight granola recipe is an easy way to make homemade cereal. Serve in a bowl with cold milk over the top or sprinkle it over your yogurt.

INGREDIENTS

4½ cups (360 g) old-fashioned rolled oats

1½ cups (182 g) chopped pecans

⅓ cup (80 ml) mild-tasting oil

6 tbsp (90 ml) honey

¼ cup (36 g) brown sugar

4 tsp (12 g) Pumpkin Pie Spice Mix (page 192)

1 tsp vanilla extract

DIRECTIONS

Preheat the oven to 350°F (177°C). Grease a 12 x 17-inch (30 x 43-cm) jelly roll pan.

In a medium bowl, combine the oats and pecans. Add the oil, honey, brown sugar, Pumpkin Pie Spice Mix and vanilla to the oats. Stir well to mix.

Press the oat mixture onto the jelly roll pan. Bake for 10 minutes. Turn off the oven—being sure not to open the oven door—and leave the oats in the oven 6 to 8 hours or overnight.

STORING
Store the granola in an airtight container for up to 1 week.

CARAMELIZED PEAR SLOW COOKER OATMEAL

There is nothing like waking up to the scent of caramelized pears to help you skip the snooze button and hop out of bed! I like to use Bartlett pears in this recipe, but you can use any crisp, sweet pear.

INGREDIENTS

2 medium pears, peeled, cored and chopped into bite-size pieces

¼ cup (36 g) brown sugar

2 tbsp (28 g) butter, melted

2 tsp (6 g) ground cinnamon

2 cups (160 g) steel cut oats

2 cups (480 ml) milk

2 cups (480 ml) water

½ cup (120 ml) Caramel Sauce (page 198)

DIRECTIONS

Add the pears, brown sugar, butter and cinnamon to a 3- to 4-quart (2.9- to 3.8-L) slow cooker. Toss to coat the pears.

Sprinkle the oats over the pears. Pour the milk and water over the oats. Do not stir.

Cook on low for 6 to 8 hours, stirring at the end of the cooking time. To serve, spoon the oatmeal into bowls. Drizzle the Caramel Sauce over the oatmeal.

NOTE

If you are using a larger slow cooker, put a bowl inside the slow cooker and place the ingredients in that bowl. Add water to the slow cooker up to the halfway mark on the bowl. This creates a water bath and will prevent your oatmeal from being scorched in the large slow cooker.

STORING AND REHEATING

Divide the oatmeal between individual microwave-safe containers. Drizzle caramel sauce over the top. Store in the refrigerator for up to 4 days or the freezer for up to a month.

Thaw frozen oatmeal in the refrigerator overnight. Reheat in the microwave for 1 to 2 minutes on high power. Stir in milk as needed to reach the desired consistency.

CINNAMON ROLL
SLOW COOKER OATMEAL

This is so tasty I could eat it for dessert. Okay, okay—this is so tasty that I do eat it for dessert. I like to put this recipe in the slow cooker on Saturday night, so we wake up to an almost-made breakfast. All I have to do is quickly make the toppings and breakfast is ready.

OATMEAL

2 cups (322 g) steel-cut oats

¼ cup (36 g) brown sugar

1 tbsp (15 ml) vanilla extract

2 cups (480 ml) milk

2 cups (480 ml) water

CINNAMON TOPPING

2 tbsp (28 g) butter, melted

3 tbsp (27 g) brown sugar

2 tsp (6 g) ground cinnamon

VANILLA ICING

1 tbsp (15 ml) milk

1 tsp vanilla extract

⅓ cup (43 g) powdered sugar

DIRECTIONS

To make the oatmeal, add the oats, brown sugar and vanilla to a 3- to 4-quart (2.9- to 3.8-L) slow cooker. Pour the milk and water over the oats. Stir to combine.

Cook the oatmeal on low for 6 to 8 hours.

When you are ready to serve the oatmeal, make the cinnamon topping and vanilla icing. To make the cinnamon topping, combine the butter, brown sugar and cinnamon in a small bowl.

To make the vanilla icing, add the milk and vanilla to a small bowl. Slowly add the powdered sugar until you reach the desired consistency.

To serve, spoon the oatmeal into bowls. Drizzle the cinnamon topping over the oatmeal, then drizzle the vanilla icing over the cinnamon topping.

NOTE

If you are using a larger slow cooker, put a bowl inside the slow cooker and place the ingredients in that bowl. Add water to the slow cooker up to the halfway mark on the bowl. This creates a water bath and will prevent your oatmeal from being scorched in the large slow cooker.

STORING AND REHEATING

Divide the oatmeal between individual microwave-safe containers. Spoon the cinnamon topping over the oatmeal. Then drizzle the icing over the top. Seal and store in the refrigerator for up to 4 days or in the freezer for up to a month.

Thaw frozen oatmeal in the refrigerator overnight. Reheat in the microwave for 1 to 2 minutes on high power. Stir in milk as needed to reach the desired consistency.

Part 2

MAKE-AHEAD LUNCHES

Mornings are stressful even without adding the burden of packing lunches to the required tasks. By making lunches ahead of time, you will save time and money while creating wholesome meals to get you through your busy day.

HOW TO PREVENT LUNCH RUTS

When many people think of meal prep, they immediately picture five of the exact same lunches sitting on the counter because they have seen that image so many times. If you want to eat the same thing each day, go for it—but there is no reason you have to. I like to choose a few recipes that have ingredients in common. I batch-cook and or prep those ingredients at the same time. This allows me to make a variety of meals to pack as lunches for my family.

TIPS FOR PACKING LUNCHES

If possible, choose an insulated lunch bag or box. This will prevent your food from warming up in transit to school or work. Add an ice pack or a frozen water bottle to keep your food cool, especially if you aren't able to refrigerate your food.

Put your food in airtight containers to keep it fresh and to keep it from leaking.

Place your salad dressing in a small container, then place that container inside the salad container. If the dressing leaks, it will leak just on your salad and not all over the lunch bag.

Place your sandwich in a sandwich box rather than a baggie to keep it from getting smashed by the other foods.

KIDS WILL EAT GROWN-UP LUNCHES

You may have to adapt your kids' lunches to the lunchroom environment (e.g., no microwaves) and school rules (e.g., no nuts), but kids enjoy many of the same meals for lunch that adults do. Save time on lunch prep by cooking recipes you can use in your kids' lunches as well as your own. If you have a child going through a picky phase, look for recipes that include the foods your child will eat, even if the items need to be prepared in a slightly different way. For instance, my youngest child went through a phase when he wanted to eat spaghetti. All. The. Time. Fortunately, he liked spaghetti-squash noodles, so I could prepare a large batch of squash noodles and use some for his spaghetti, while the rest could be used in a variety of lunch bowls for the rest of the family.

HOT LUNCH OR COLD LUNCH

Some of the recipes in the lunch section can be served either hot or cold. A few are best when served warm and most of the salads are best served cold. Evaluate your lunchtime setting and your work schedule before you make your lunches for the week. Do you have access to a microwave? If not, you will want to skip the meals that are best served warm. Will you have to eat lunch at your desk while working or will you need to eat on the go? Then choose a lunch that you can just grab and eat. The success of make-ahead lunches depends on two things: (1) your finding time to actually make the lunches ahead of time and (2) choosing meals that best fit into your lunch environment and schedule.

Chapter 4

ONE-BOWL WONDERS

Many of these one-bowl wonders are based on our favorite dinner recipes. If you have difficulty finding time to fit a meal-prep day into your busy schedule, I recommend starting by making a double batch of one of the one-bowl wonder recipes. Serve half for dinner, then use the rest to create lunch bowls. Put a couple bowls in the refrigerator to use and freeze the rest for later. If you do this a couple days a week, it won't be long before you have a freezer stocked with pre-made lunches.

ALTERNATIVES TO RICE BOWLS

We enjoy rice and pasta as a filler in many of our lunch dishes. However, cooked rice and pasta continue to absorb liquid while sitting in your lunch box, which changes the texture of the dish as well as the rice and pasta.

I have found that my family enjoys spaghetti squash, quinoa and cauliflower rice in place of traditional pasta and rice. Spaghetti squash, quinoa and cauliflower rice hold up better, stay firmer and do not become mushy in a lunch box. They also have fewer carbohydrates, so they don't contribute to the afternoon slump.

TIPS FOR PACKING LUNCH BOWLS

The bowls work best when they are packed in a sealable bowl made from microwave-safe material. I usually use a tempered glass container with a silicone lid. But there are a variety of products out there that will work.

Place the rice, noodles or quinoa on the bottom as the base of the dish. Then place the meat and vegetables on top. This allows the juices from the meat and vegetables to trickle down and flavor the rice, noodles or quinoa.

Allow the bowls to cool off completely before freezing them. This will prevent ice crystals from forming on the food. You can place a piece of plastic wrap over the top of the food, pressing down to seal the air out of the food, before placing the lid on the container and freezing; but remember to remove the plastic wrap before you reheat the bowl.

Most of these lunch bowl recipes will keep in the refrigerator for up to five days. However, if you use rice, I recommend storing it in the refrigerator for only three days. Fortunately, rice bowls freeze well.

If possible, thaw the frozen lunch bowls overnight in the refrigerator. They may still be frozen when you pack them in the morning but should be mostly, if not completely, thawed by lunchtime.

If you will not be able to refrigerate your lunch bowls at work or school, pack them in an insulated lunch bag with an ice pack.

HOW TO BATCH-COOK CAULIFLOWER RICE

Don't turn your nose up at cauliflower rice until you have tried it. It has a mild flavor and easily picks up the flavors of the dish you serve it with. Unlike traditional rice, it doesn't absorb the liquid in a dish, so cauliflower rice is ideal for make-ahead meals that are stored in the refrigerator for several days.

HOW TO RICE CAULIFLOWER IN A FOOD PROCESSOR

Discard the stem and leaves and chop the cauliflower into florets. Place the cauliflower pieces in the processor. Don't fill the food processor more than three-quarters full. You can do multiple batches if necessary.

Pulse the food processor in 1-second pulses until it has completely broken down the cauliflower into rice-size pieces. If you find any large pieces after you remove the cauliflower rice from the food processor, simply place them back in the processor and pulse until they are broken down.

HOW TO RICE CAULIFLOWER IN A BLENDER

Discard the stem and leaves and chop the cauliflower into florets. Place the cauliflower pieces in the blender, keeping them 1 inch (3 cm) below the max fill line.

Add water to the blender, covering the cauliflower completely. Do not exceed the max fill line. Pulse the blender repeatedly until you no longer see any large pieces of cauliflower. Pour the cauliflower into a strainer to drain all the water. Pat dry, then use it as called for in a recipe or store.

HOW TO RICE CAULIFLOWER WITHOUT A FOOD PROCESSOR OR BLENDER

If you do not have a food processor or blender, you can use a box grater or even a knife to rice your cauliflower. It is time-consuming, but effective.

Now that cauliflower has become popular, you can also find raw riced cauliflower in the produce section of your grocery store and possibly even the freezer section.

HOW TO STORE RAW CAULIFLOWER RICE

If you are not going to use the cauliflower immediately after ricing it, place it in a sealable bag and remove the excess air. Store it in the refrigerator for up to 3 days or the freezer for up to 3 months.

HOW TO STORE COOKED CAULIFLOWER RICE

Store cooked cauliflower rice in airtight containers or freezer bags. Cooked cauliflower rice will keep in the refrigerator for up to 5 days and in the freezer for up to 6 months. I usually store my cooked cauliflower rice in 2-, 3- or 4-cup (421-, 632- or 842-g) quantities, so I have the right amount for different recipes.

Thaw frozen cauliflower rice in the refrigerator overnight. If you have stored your cauliflower rice in a microwave-safe container, you can also thaw it in the microwave by cooking it on high power for 3 to 4 minutes.

HOW TO BATCH-COOK CAULIFLOWER RICE ON THE STOVE TOP

INGREDIENTS

1 tbsp (15 ml) olive oil

2 lb (900 g) cauliflower rice

DIRECTIONS

Heat the oil in a large skillet over medium-high heat. Add the cauliflower rice and cook, stirring occasionally, until the cauliflower rice is tender, approximately 5 minutes.

HOW TO BATCH-COOK CAULIFLOWER RICE IN THE OVEN

INGREDIENTS

2 lb (900 g) cauliflower rice

2 tbsp (30 ml) olive oil

DIRECTIONS

Preheat the oven to 425°F (218°C). Spread the cauliflower rice out on a large baking sheet. Drizzle it with the oil. Toss to coat. Bake for 15 to 17 minutes, or until the cauliflower rice is a light golden brown.

VEGETABLE FRIED CAULIFLOWER RICE

Warning: this is addicting. Fortunately, fried cauliflower rice has so many fewer calories and carbs than traditional fried rice, you can help yourself to seconds without feeling guilty. You can use this as a base in any of the Asian-flavored lunch bowls.

INGREDIENTS

2 tbsp (30 ml) sesame oil, divided

4 large eggs, beaten

2 lb (900 g) raw cauliflower rice (pages 86–87)

8 green onions, thinly sliced

1 clove garlic, minced

1 cup (151 g) frozen peas and carrots

6 tbsp (90 ml) soy sauce

2 tbsp (30 ml) orange juice

2 tbsp (30 ml) honey

Pinch of salt

1 cup (270 g) fresh bean sprouts

DIRECTIONS

Heat 1 tablespoon (15 ml) of the oil in a large skillet over medium heat. Add the eggs and scramble them for approximately 5 minutes. Set aside.

Heat the remaining 1 tablespoon (15 ml) oil in the skillet over medium-high heat. Add the cauliflower rice, green onions, garlic and peas and carrots. Cook for 4 to 5 minutes, or until the green onions are tender.

Add the soy sauce, orange juice, honey, salt and bean sprouts to the skillet. Cook, stirring, for 3 minutes, or until most of the liquid has been absorbed and the sprouts are tender. Stir in the scrambled eggs. Toss to coat and cook until the eggs are heated through, about 2 to 3 minutes.

STORING AND REHEATING

Store cooked cauliflower rice in an airtight container or sealable freezer bag in the refrigerator for up to 5 days or in the freezer for up to 6 months.

Thaw frozen cauliflower rice in the refrigerator overnight.

To reheat cauliflower rice on the stove, put it in a saucepan with 1 tablespoon (15 ml) of water. Cover and cook over low heat, stirring occasionally, until it is heated through, approximately 10 minutes.

To reheat cauliflower rice in a microwave, put it in a microwave-safe dish, cover it with a damp paper towel and microwave on high for 2 minutes. Stir and check to see if it is heated through. If not, keep heating it in 1-minute increments until it is heated through.

HOW TO BATCH-COOK QUINOA

Quinoa comes in a variety of colors, and though the flavor of each variety is slightly different, the preparation is the same for all of them. There are a variety of methods for cooking quinoa, but the ratio of dried quinoa to liquid remains the same: one part quinoa to two parts liquid. You can cook the quinoa in water or broth.

HOW TO STORE COOKED QUINOA

Store cooked quinoa in airtight containers or freezer bags. Cooked quinoa will keep in the refrigerator for up to 5 days and in the freezer for up to 6 months. I usually store my cooked quinoa in 2- to 3-cup (322- to 483-g) quantities, so I have the right amount for different recipes.

Thaw frozen quinoa in the refrigerator overnight. If you have stored your quinoa in a microwave-safe container, you can also thaw it in the microwave by cooking it on high power for 3 to 4 minutes.

HOW TO BATCH-COOK QUINOA ON THE STOVE TOP

INGREDIENTS

2 cups (360 g) quinoa

4 cups (960 ml) water

DIRECTIONS

Add the quinoa and water to a large pot with a lid. Cook the quinoa over medium-high heat until it reaches a boil. Place the lid on the pot, reduce the heat to low and simmer for 10 to 15 minutes, or until the germ separates from the seed.

HOW TO BATCH-COOK QUINOA IN A SLOW COOKER

INGREDIENTS

2 cups (360 g) quinoa

4 cups (960 ml) water

DIRECTIONS

Add the quinoa and water to a slow cooker. Place the lid on the slow cooker and cook for 5 to 6 hours on low or 3 to 4 hours on high, or until the germ separates from the seed.

HOW TO BATCH-COOK QUINOA IN A PRESSURE COOKER

INGREDIENTS

2 cups (360 g) quinoa

4 cups (960 ml) water

DIRECTIONS

Place the quinoa and water in the pressure cooker. Seal the lid and cook on high pressure for 6 minutes, or until the germ separates from the seed. Use the quick-release method to release the steam.

GREEK QUINOA

My family enjoys this quinoa enough to make a meal of it alone. This pairs well with the Mediterranean Chicken and Vegetable Bowl (page 105). But you can also add it to a bowl and stir in some raw vegetables for a simple lunch.

INGREDIENTS

3 cups (483 g) cooked quinoa (page 90)

3 tbsp (45 ml) red wine vinegar

2 tbsp + 1 tsp (35 ml) olive oil

1 tsp dried oregano

1 tsp dried basil

1 tsp garlic powder

½ tsp Dijon mustard

½ tsp onion powder

¼ tsp Seasoned Salt (page 191)

Pinch of coarsely ground pepper

DIRECTIONS

Add the quinoa to a medium pot.

In a small bowl, combine the vinegar, oil, oregano, basil, garlic powder, mustard, onion powder, Seasoned Salt and pepper. Mix well. Pour it over the quinoa and toss to thoroughly coat.

Cook over medium-low heat until the quinoa is heated through, approximately 5 minutes.

STORING AND REHEATING

Store cooked quinoa in an airtight container or sealable freezer bag in the refrigerator for up to 5 days or in the freezer for up to 6 months.

Thaw frozen quinoa in the refrigerator overnight.

To reheat quinoa on the stove top, put it in a saucepan with 1 tablespoon (15 ml) of water. Cover and cook over low heat, stirring occasionally, until it is heated through, approximately 10 minutes.

To reheat quinoa in a microwave, put it in a microwave-safe dish, cover it with a damp paper towel and microwave on high for 2 minutes. Stir and check to see if it is heated through. If not, keep heating it in 1-minute increments until it is heated through.

CILANTRO-LIME QUINOA

This makes a tasty substitution for rice in Southwestern dishes. Cup for cup, quinoa has about the same number of calories as rice. However, quinoa has more fiber and protein per serving than rice. So substituting quinoa for rice in dishes is an easy way to increase your fiber and protein intake without compromising on flavor.

INGREDIENTS

3 cups (483 g) cooked quinoa (page 90)

1 tbsp (15 ml) olive oil

4 tsp (20 ml) lime juice

Zest of 1 lime

⅓ cup (13 g) fresh cilantro, chopped

DIRECTIONS

Add the quinoa to a medium pot.

Combine the oil, lime juice, lime zest and cilantro in a small bowl. Pour this mixture over the quinoa. Toss to coat.

Cook over medium-low heat until the quinoa is heated through, approximately 5 minutes.

STORING AND REHEATING

Store cooked quinoa in an airtight container or sealable freezer bag in the refrigerator for up to 5 days or in the freezer for up to 6 months.

Thaw frozen quinoa in the refrigerator overnight.

To reheat quinoa on the stove top, put it in a saucepan with 1 tablespoon (15 ml) of water. Cover and cook over low heat, stirring occasionally, until it is heated through, approximately 10 minutes.

To reheat quinoa in a microwave, put it in a microwave-safe dish, cover it with a damp paper towel and microwave on high for 2 minutes. Stir and check to see if it is heated through. If not, keep heating it in 1-minute increments until it is heated through.

HOW TO BATCH-COOK SPAGHETTI SQUASH

Unless you roast them in the oven, it is hard to batch-cook spaghetti squash because they are so large. However, the pressure cooker and microwave are so fast that you can cook several spaghetti squashes in a row.

HOW TO STORE COOKED SPAGHETTI SQUASH

Store cooked spaghetti squash in airtight containers or freezer bags. Cooked spaghetti squash will keep in the refrigerator for up to 5 days and in the freezer for up to 6 months. I usually store my cooked spaghetti squash in 4-, 5- or 6-cup (720-g, 900-g or 1-kg) quantities, so I have the right amount for different recipes.

Thaw frozen spaghetti squash in the refrigerator overnight. If you have stored your spaghetti squash in a microwave-safe container, you can also thaw it in the microwave.

HOW TO BATCH-COOK SPAGHETTI SQUASH IN THE OVEN

INGREDIENTS

1 to 3 (4- to 6-lb [1.8- to 2.7-kg]) spaghetti squashes

Olive oil

DIRECTIONS

Preheat the oven to 400°F (204°C).

Cut the stems off the spaghetti squashes. Place the cut side down and cut the squashes in half. Scoop the seeds out of the insides of the spaghetti squashes.

Brush the squashes' flesh with oil and place them cut-side down on a large baking sheet. Place the baking sheet in the oven and roast the squashes for 30 minutes, or until a fork easily punctures them.

Use a fork to loosen and remove the squash "noodles."

HOW TO BATCH-COOK SPAGHETTI SQUASH IN THE SLOW COOKER

INGREDIENTS

1 (4- to 6-lb [1.8- to 2.7-kg]) spaghetti squash

1 cup (240 ml) vegetable broth or water

DIRECTIONS

With a sharp knife, cut a few slits in the spaghetti squash. Be sure to make them deep enough that the steam can be released from inside the squash.

Place the whole squash in a large slow cooker. Cover and cook on high for 3 to 4 hours or on low for 6 to 8 hours.

Cut the squash in half. Scrape out the seeds. Use a fork to loosen and remove the squash "noodles."

HOW TO BATCH-COOK SPAGHETTI SQUASH IN THE PRESSURE COOKER

INGREDIENTS

1 (3- to 4-lb [1.4- to 1.8-kg])
spaghetti squash

1 cup (240 ml) water

DIRECTIONS

Cut the stem off the spaghetti squash. Place the cut side down and cut the squash in half. Scoop the seeds out of the spaghetti squash.

Add the water to the pressure cooker and insert the rack. Place the spaghetti squash on the rack or in a steamer basket in the pressure cooker. Cook for 8 minutes on high pressure. Use the quick-release method to release the steam.

Use a fork to loosen and remove the squash "noodles."

HOW TO BATCH-COOK SPAGHETTI SQUASH IN THE MICROWAVE

INGREDIENTS

1 (3½- to 5-lb [1.6- to 2.3-kg])
spaghetti squash

DIRECTIONS

With a sharp knife, cut a few slits in the spaghetti squash. Be sure to make them deep enough that the steam can be released from inside the squash.

Place the whole squash in the microwave. Cook on full power for 12 minutes. Check the squash after 12 minutes. If it isn't soft to the touch, cook it on high for another 2 to 3 minutes. The squash will become very soft to the touch when it is done.

Once the squash is cool enough for you to touch it, cut off the stem end, then cut the squash in half lengthwise. Scoop out the seeds and the pulp that easily comes out with the seeds.

Use a fork to loosen and remove the squash "noodles."

GARLIC BUTTER SPAGHETTI SQUASH NOODLES

This is pure comfort food. Even better is the fact that you can indulge in this comfort food without having to worry about the carbs in traditional pasta. This can be eaten on its own, as a side dish or as a base in a wonder bowl.

INGREDIENTS

1 (4- to 6-lb [1.8- to 2.7-kg]) cooked spaghetti squash (pages 94–95)

3 tbsp (42 g) butter

3 tbsp (45 ml) olive oil

1 tbsp (9 g) minced garlic

2 tsp (2 g) dried parsley

1 tsp dried basil

¼ tsp Seasoned Salt (page 191)

DIRECTIONS

Add the spaghetti squash to a large bowl.

Combine the butter, oil, garlic, parsley, basil and Seasoned Salt in a medium pot. Cook over a medium heat until the butter is melted. Stir in the squash noodles. Cook over a medium-low heat until the squash noodles are heated through, approximately 5 minutes.

STORING AND REHEATING

Store the cooked spaghetti squash noodles in an airtight container or sealable freezer bag in the refrigerator for up to 5 days or in the freezer for up to 6 months.

Thaw frozen spaghetti squash noodles in the refrigerator overnight.

To reheat spaghetti squash noodles on the stove top, add a tablespoon (15 ml) of olive oil to a large skillet. Add the squash noodles and cook over a medium-low heat, stirring frequently, until the noodles are heated through, approximately 5 to 7 minutes.

To reheat spaghetti squash noodles in a microwave, place them in a microwave-safe dish, cover with a damp paper towel and microwave on high for 1 minute. Stir and check to see if it is heated through. If not, keep heating it in 1-minute increments until it is heated through.

MONGOLIAN BEEF AND BROCCOLI BOWL

Serves 5

Mongolian Beef and Broccoli is a bolder, spicier and yet sweeter version of traditional beef and broccoli. While I stated earlier that you don't have to eat the same lunch every day of the week, you might want to after you try this.

This is delicious over plain rice, but you can also serve it over Vegetable Fried Cauliflower Rice (page 88).

INGREDIENTS

1 tbsp (15 ml) olive oil

¼ cup (34 g) diced onion

1½ lb (675 g) steak, cut into bite-size pieces

2 cloves garlic, minced

¼ cup (60 ml) water

4 tsp (12 g) cornstarch

¼ cup (60 ml) soy sauce

¼ cup (60 ml) beef broth

⅓ cup + 1 tbsp (57 g) brown sugar

½ tsp ground ginger

½ tsp red pepper flakes

1 lb (450 g) broccoli florets

2½ cups (402 g) cooked rice

DIRECTIONS

Heat oil in a large skillet over medium-high heat. Add the onion and steak and sauté until the meat is browned, approximately 5 minutes. Add the garlic and cook for 1 minute.

In a small bowl, whisk together the water and cornstarch. Add the soy sauce, broth, brown sugar, ginger and red pepper flakes. Stir well to combine.

Pour the sauce over the beef and add the broccoli. Stir to coat the beef and broccoli with the sauce. Reduce the heat to medium-low and cook until the sauce is thick and bubbly, approximately 5 minutes.

Divide the cooked rice between 5 lidded, microwave-safe bowls. Spoon the Mongolian Beef and Broccoli over the rice.

STORING AND REHEATING

Seal each bowl and store in the refrigerator for up to 3 days or the freezer for up to 3 months. Thaw overnight in the refrigerator.

Reheat a thawed bowl in a microwave on high power for 1 minute.

Reheat a frozen bowl in a microwave on 50 percent power for 3 to 4 minutes. Stir, then cook 30 seconds on high power to heat it through.

BOURBON BEEF
AND QUINOA BOWL

Yes, I realize this is a lunch recipe. Don't worry—the alcohol is cooked off and you are left with a deep, rich sauce for your beef and green beans.

INGREDIENTS

¼ cup (60 ml) bourbon

¼ cup (36 g) brown sugar

¼ cup (60 ml) beef broth

2 tbsp (30 ml) soy sauce

1 tbsp (15 ml) Worcestershire sauce

½ cup (68 g) diced onion

1½ lb (675 g) steak, cut into bite-size pieces

1 lb (450 g) frozen green beans, thawed

2½ cups (403 g) cooked quinoa (page 90)

DIRECTIONS

Add the bourbon, brown sugar, broth, soy sauce and Worcestershire sauce to a large skillet, stirring to combine. Turn on the heat to medium-high. Add the onion and steak. Toss to coat, then sauté until the steak is browned on all sides, approximately 5 minutes.

Add the green beans and toss to coat. Lower the heat to medium. Cook until the green beans are fork-tender and the steak is cooked through, approximately 8 minutes.

Place ½ cup (81 g) of quinoa in each of 5 lidded, microwave-safe bowls. Divide the steak and green beans between the bowls.

STORING AND REHEATING

Seal each bowl and store in the refrigerator for up to 5 days or the freezer for up to 3 months. Thaw overnight in the refrigerator.

Reheat a thawed bowl in a microwave on high power for 1 minute.

Reheat a frozen bowl in a microwave on 50 percent power for 3 to 4 minutes. Stir then cook 30 seconds on high power to heat it through.

CAJUN RANCH CHICKEN AND QUINOA BOWLS WITH CHOPPED KALE

This chicken bowl has a little kick to it. The kale is tossed with a Cajun ranch dressing before being added to the bowl. If you don't have kale, substitute another hardy green (like Swiss chard) that can handle being soaked in dressing without wilting; or put your dressing in a separate container and add it to the salad right before eating.

INGREDIENTS

1 tbsp (15 ml) olive oil

½ cup (68 g) diced onion

½ cup (85 g) diced red or green bell pepper

1¼ lb (563 g) boneless, skinless chicken thighs or breasts, cut into bite-size pieces

1 tbsp + 2 tsp (15 g) Cajun Seasoning Mix (page 190), divided

½ cup (120 ml) Ranch Salad Dressing (page 194)

5 cups (180 g) chopped kale

2½ cups (403 g) cooked quinoa (page 90)

DIRECTIONS

Heat the oil in a large skillet over medium heat. Add the onion and bell pepper and sauté until the onion is translucent, approximately 5 minutes. Add the chicken and 1 tablespoon (9 g) of the Cajun Seasoning Mix. Cook until the chicken is cooked through, approximately 10 minutes.

In a small bowl, whisk together the Ranch Salad Dressing and the remaining 2 teaspoons (6 g) of Cajun Seasoning Mix. Toss the kale in a large bowl with enough of the Cajun ranch dressing to lightly coat the kale.

To make the bowls, place 1 cup (36 g) of kale in one-half of each of 5 lidded bowls. Place ½ cup (81 g) of quinoa in the other half of the bowls. Divide the Cajun chicken between the bowls and place it on top of the quinoa.

Drizzle any remaining dressing over each bowl.

STORING

Seal each bowl and store in the refrigerator for up to 5 days. Serve cold.

If you would like to freeze the bowls, add just the quinoa and Cajun chicken to the bowl and freeze. Thaw overnight in the refrigerator. Once the bowl is thawed, add the fresh greens and top it with the dressing.

MEDITERRANEAN CHICKEN AND VEGETABLE BOWL

Serves 5

I throw around the word "Mediterranean" when cooking just to have an excuse to add artichokes and olives to a dish. I buy packages of frozen artichoke hearts whenever I go to Trader Joe's. They are inexpensive compared to canned artichokes, and they don't have any kind of seasoning, so they take on the flavors of the dish they are added to.

You can serve this dish over rice or noodles, but it is especially delicious when served with Greek Quinoa (page 91).

INGREDIENTS

3 tbsp (45 ml) olive oil, divided

1½ lb (675 g) boneless, skinless chicken thighs or breasts, cut into bite-size pieces

¼ cup (34 g) diced red onion

3 cloves garlic, minced

4 tbsp (60 ml) red wine vinegar

1 tbsp (9 g) Italian Seasoning Mix (page 191)

½ tsp Dijon mustard

12 oz (340 g) frozen artichoke hearts, thawed

1 (3.8-oz [106-g]) can sliced black olives, drained

1¾ cups (282 g) fresh diced tomatoes or 1 (15-oz [424-g]) can diced tomatoes, drained

2½ cups (403 g) cooked quinoa (page 90)

DIRECTIONS

Heat 1 tablespoon (15 ml) of the oil in a large skillet over medium-high heat. Add the chicken, onion and garlic. Cook until the onion is translucent and the chicken is browned, approximately 5 minutes.

In a small bowl, combine the remaining 2 tablespoons (30 ml) of oil, vinegar, Italian Seasoning Mix and mustard. Add this mixture to the chicken.

Add the artichoke hearts and olives. Toss to coat. Lower the heat to medium and cook until the chicken is cooked through, approximately 10 minutes.

To make the bowls, add ½ cup (81 g) of cooked quinoa to each of 5 lidded, microwave-safe bowls. Spoon the chicken and vegetables over the quinoa.

STORING AND REHEATING

Seal each bowl and store in the refrigerator for up to 5 days or the freezer for up to 3 months. Thaw overnight in the refrigerator.

Reheat a thawed bowl in a microwave on high power for 1 minute.

Reheat a frozen bowl in a microwave on 50 percent power for 3 to 4 minutes. Stir then cook 30 seconds on high power to heat it through.

TURKEY TACO RICE BOWL

A few years ago, my friend Tegan VandenBosch introduced me to the idea of adding diced tomatoes directly to taco meat. The meat takes on the flavor of the tomatoes and the tomatoes pick up the spices. It is a delicious combination that speeds up prep time.

If you prefer to not use rice, you can substitute Cilantro-Lime Quinoa (page 92).

INGREDIENTS

2½ cups (402 g) cooked rice

1 tbsp (15 ml) olive oil

1 to 1½ lb (450 to 675 g) ground turkey

¼ cup (34 g) diced onion

3 tbsp (27 g) Taco Seasoning Mix (page 190), divided

1¾ cups (282 g) fresh diced tomatoes or 1 (15-oz [424-g]) can diced tomatoes, drained

1½ cups (302 g) cooked black beans or 1 (15-oz [424-g]) can black beans, drained and rinsed

1 (15-oz [424-g]) can corn, drained

¾ cup (98 g) shredded Monterey Jack cheese

¾ cup (180 ml) salsa, optional

DIRECTIONS

Place ½ cup (81 g) of rice in each of 5 lidded, microwave-safe bowls.

Heat the oil in a large skillet over medium-high heat. Add the ground turkey and onion and sauté until the onion has softened, about 5 minutes. Add 2 tablespoons (18 g) of the Taco Seasoning Mix and the diced tomatoes and cook for 5 minutes, or until the meat is cooked through. Divide the meat and tomato mixture between the bowls. Leave 1 tablespoon (15 ml) of the cooking liquid in the skillet.

Add the beans and corn to the skillet. Sprinkle the remaining 1 tablespoon (9 g) of the Taco Seasoning Mix over the beans and corn and toss to coat. Reduce the heat to medium-low and cook until the corn and beans are heated through, approximately 5 minutes. Divide the corn and bean mixture between the bowls.

Sprinkle the Monterey Jack over the bowls. Serve the taco bowls with salsa if desired.

STORING AND REHEATING

Seal each bowl and store in the refrigerator for up to 3 days or the freezer for up to 3 months. Thaw overnight in the refrigerator.

Reheat a thawed bowl in a microwave on high power for 1 minute.

Reheat a frozen bowl in a microwave on 50 percent power for 3 to 4 minutes. Stir then cook 30 seconds on high power to heat it through.

SALMON-BERRY QUINOA BOWL

This bowl is the ultimate superfood lunch bowl: salmon, berries, quinoa and kale. However, when I created this combo with my dad, we were thinking about the flavors rather than the health benefits. Feel free to ignore how healthy this dish is and instead savor the raspberry-balsamic dressing drizzled over this dish.

DRESSING

¼ cup (55 g) raspberry jam

¼ cup (60 ml) balsamic vinegar

¼ cup (60 ml) olive oil

2 tsp (8 g) sugar

1 tsp ground mustard

Dash of coarsely ground pepper

SALMON

2 tbsp (28 g) raspberry jam

1 tbsp + 1½ tsp (23 ml) balsamic vinegar

1½ lb (675 g) salmon

3 cups (483 g) cooked quinoa (page 90)

3 cups (108 g) chopped kale

1½ cups (149 g) fresh blackberries

1½ cups (149 g) fresh blueberries

DIRECTIONS

Preheat the oven to 400°F (204°C).

To make the dressing, combine the raspberry jam, vinegar, oil, sugar, ground mustard and pepper in a medium cruet or lidded jar. Shake well to mix.

To make the salmon, combine the raspberry jam and vinegar in a small bowl.

Place the salmon, skin-side down, in a medium baking dish. Spoon the jam mixture over the salmon.

Bake the salmon for 10 to 15 minutes, or until it is cooked through and easily flakes with a fork. Cut the salmon into 5 pieces. Remove the meat from the skin when you lift the portions from the baking dish.

To make the bowls, add ½ cup (81 g) of quinoa to each of 5 lidded bowls. Divide the kale between the bowls then add the blackberries, blueberries and salmon. Drizzle the dressing over the bowls.

STORING

Seal each bowl and store in the refrigerator for up to 3 days. Serve cold.

If you would like to freeze the bowls, add just the quinoa and salmon to the bowls and freeze. Thaw overnight in the refrigerator. Once a bowl is thawed, add the kale and berries. Top with the dressing.

ZUCCHINI PARMESAN BOWL WITH SPAGHETTI SQUASH

I call this recipe a bowl, but I usually pack it in a 7 x 4-inch (18 x 10-cm) rectangular glass container, because the zucchini slices fit better. The one vegetable my husband doesn't like is eggplant, so I compromise and broil zucchini for this dish instead. It is slathered in spaghetti sauce and cooked with cheese, so I don't miss the eggplant. If you miss the breading, try adding croutons to the dish.

INGREDIENTS

2 small zucchini, cut into ½-inch (13-mm) thick slices lengthwise

2 tbsp (30 ml) olive oil

5 cups (900 g) cooked spaghetti squash (pages 94–95)

1¼ cups (300 ml) Spaghetti Sauce (page 195)

1 cup (130 g) shredded mozzarella cheese

½ cup (90 g) grated Parmesan cheese

1 cup (121 g) Italian Seasoned Croutons (page 197) (optional)

DIRECTIONS

Preheat the oven to broil. Line a medium baking sheet with foil.

Arrange the zucchini slices in one layer on the baking sheet. Brush both sides of the zucchini slices with the oil.

Place the baking sheet in the oven 4 inches (10 cm) below the heat source. Broil for 3 minutes, or until the tops of the slices are browned. Turn the slices over and broil for 3 minutes more.

To make the bowls, divide the cooked spaghetti squash between each of 5 lidded, microwave-safe, oven-safe bowls. Place the broiled zucchini on top of the spaghetti squash. Top the zucchini slices with the Spaghetti Sauce. Sprinkle the sauce with the mozzarella, Parmesan and Italian Seasoned Croutons.

STORING AND REHEATING

Seal each bowl and store in the refrigerator for up to 3 days or in the freezer for up to 3 months. Thaw overnight in the refrigerator.

To serve, heat a bowl in the microwave on high for 1 to 1½ minutes (or bake at 375°F [191°C] for 10 minutes, or until the cheeses are melted and bubbly).

SHERRY PORK WITH BACON AND BRUSSELS SPROUTS

If you think you don't like Brussels sprouts, it's because you have never had them cooked in sherry and bacon.

Instead of cooking the bacon then crumbling it, I use kitchen scissors to cut the raw bacon into small pieces. Then it can stay in the pan and I can use the bacon grease in place of oil to cook the other ingredients.

INGREDIENTS

4 slices bacon, cut into small pieces

1 cup (135 g) chopped red onion

1½ lb (675 g) pork, cut into bite-size pieces

4 cloves garlic, minced

¼ cup (60 ml) sherry

1 tbsp (10 g) cornstarch

¼ cup (60 ml) red wine vinegar

¼ cup (36 g) brown sugar

1 lb (450 g) Brussels sprouts, cut in half

2 cups (133 g) sliced mushrooms

3 cups (483 g) cooked rice

DIRECTIONS

Cook the bacon for approximately 10 minutes in a large skillet over medium-low heat. When the bacon is mostly cooked, add the onion and pork. Increase the heat to medium-high and cook until the pork is browned on all sides, approximately 5 minutes. Add the garlic and cook for 1 minute.

In a small bowl, whisk the sherry and cornstarch together. Add the vinegar and brown sugar. Stir to combine, then pour the mixture over the pork. Add the Brussels sprouts and toss to coat. Reduce the heat to medium and cook for 8 minutes. Add the mushrooms and toss to coat. Reduce the heat to medium-low and cook for 3 to 4 minutes, or until the Brussels sprouts are fork-tender and the pork is cooked through.

Divide the cooked rice between each of 6 lidded, microwave-safe bowls. Spoon the pork and Brussels sprouts over the rice.

STORING AND REHEATING

Seal each bowl and store in the refrigerator for up to 3 days or the freezer for up to 3 months. Thaw overnight in the refrigerator.

Reheat a thawed bowl in a microwave on high power for 1 minute.

Reheat a frozen bowl in a microwave on 50 percent power for 3 to 4 minutes. Stir then cook 30 seconds on high power to heat it through.

CAPRESE SPAGHETTI SQUASH BOWL

This is basically a salad disguised as a pasta bowl. Instead of using traditional pasta, the tomato, mozzarella cheese and basil are served over spaghetti squash and then drizzled with a balsamic reduction.

BALSAMIC REDUCTION

1 cup (240 ml) balsamic vinegar

¼ cup (60 ml) honey

CAPRESE SPAGHETTI SQUASH

5 cups (900 g) cooked spaghetti squash (pages 94-95)

2½ cups (402 g) cherry tomatoes

1¼ cups (163 g) cubed mozzarella cheese

25 fresh basil leaves, shredded

DIRECTIONS

To make the balsamic reduction, combine the vinegar and honey in a small pot over medium heat. Cook until the mixture reaches a boil. Reduce the heat to low and simmer until the mixture has been reduced to about ⅓ cup (80 ml), approximately 30 minutes.

To make the Caprese Spaghetti Squash, place 1 cup (180 g) of spaghetti squash in each of 5 lidded bowls. Add ½ cup (80 g) of cherry tomatoes to each bowl. Top the tomatoes with ¼ cup (33 g) of mozzarella. Top the tomatoes with the basil. Drizzle the balsamic reduction over the bowls.

STORING

Seal each bowl and store in the refrigerator for 3 to 5 days, depending on the freshness of the tomatoes and basil. Serve cold.

Chapter 5

SALADS ON THE GO

The salads in this chapter are hearty and are meant to be stand-alone meals, but you can pack a small serving to use as a side salad. I have used ingredients that can stand up to five days in the refrigerator as well as travel well.

You can cover and store these salads in the bowl in which you make them then pack a serving each day for your lunch. However, if you have enough lunch containers, you can divide them up immediately, so all you have to do is grab a container each morning for your lunch.

TIPS FOR PREVENTING WILTED GREENS

Many lettuces wilt when exposed to dressings or the juices from other vegetables. There are a couple things you can do to prevent the greens from wilting.

First, you can use firmer greens—such as kale, Swiss chard or cabbage—that can better stand up to liquids.

Don't pack your lunches in canning jars. I know they are pretty, but they aren't very practical and they smash your greens. Use a large salad container that doesn't compress your greens.

Limit the juices from other ingredients. Use whole cherry tomatoes instead of diced tomatoes. Use vegetables with a lower water content, such as carrots, broccoli, celery and snap peas.

Don't add the dressing until just before serving. You can store your dressing in a separate container.

Cool cooked items (such as rice, beans, lentils and meat) before adding them to your salad.

You can also layer your salad, so the dressing is separated from the lettuces by a layer of nonabsorbent ingredients, such as firm vegetables, cheese or meat.

CHOPPED CHIMICHURRI
STEAK SALAD

I took the basic ingredients for a chimichurri sauce and turned them into a dressing for this chopped salad. Don't be put off by the number of ingredients in the chimichurri dressing—it is actually very easy to make since you throw them all in a food processor or blender.

CHIMICHURRI DRESSING

1 cup (40 g) loosely packed fresh parsley leaves

1 cup (40 g) loosely packed fresh cilantro leaves

½ cup (120 ml) water

¼ cup (34 g) chopped onion

2 tbsp (30 ml) olive oil

1 tbsp (15 ml) distilled white vinegar

1 tbsp (15 ml) lime juice

1 tbsp (3 g) fresh basil or 1 tsp dried basil

1 tbsp (3 g) fresh oregano or 1 tsp dried oregano

1 tbsp (3 g) fresh thyme or 1 tsp dried thyme

2 tsp (10 ml) honey

4 cloves garlic

¼ tsp cayenne

Pinch of Seasoned Salt (page 191)

STEAK AND SALAD

1 tbsp (15 ml) olive oil

1½ lb (675 g) steak, cut into bite-size pieces

6 cups (216 g) chopped kale or romaine lettuce

1 (15-oz [424-g]) can corn, drained

1¾ cups (351 g) cooked black beans or 1 (15-oz [424-g]) can black beans, drained and rinsed

2 cups (320 g) cherry tomatoes

1 medium green bell pepper, diced

½ cup (68 g) diced red onion

DIRECTIONS

To make the chimichurri dressing, combine the parsley, cilantro, water, onion, oil, vinegar, lime juice, basil, oregano, thyme, honey, garlic, cayenne and Seasoned Salt in a food processor or blender. Puree until smooth.

To make the steak, heat the oil in a medium skillet over medium-high heat. Add the steak and cook until it is browned on all sides, approximately 5 minutes. Reduce the heat to medium-low and cook for 4 to 5 minutes, or until the steak is cooked through and the juices run clear. Remove the steak from the heat and let it rest for 5 minutes.

Add the kale, corn, beans, tomatoes, bell pepper and onion to a large bowl. Add the steak once it has cooled. Toss to combine. Drizzle the dressing over the salad. Toss to coat.

STORING

Either cover and store the salad in the large bowl or divide the salad between 6 lidded containers. Store in the refrigerator for up to 5 days.

LEMON-DIJON CHICKEN PASTA SALAD

The bright citrus dressing adds a lively flavor to this easy salad: the pasta soaks up the Lemon-Dijon Dressing, making this an especially flavorful dish.

LEMON-DIJON DRESSING

3 tbsp (45 ml) lemon juice

3 tbsp (45 ml) Dijon mustard

3 tbsp (45 ml) olive oil

3 tbsp (45 ml) honey

½ tsp dried rosemary

⅛ tsp coarsely ground pepper

SALAD

12 oz (340 g) rotini pasta

1 tbsp (15 ml) olive oil

1 lb (450 g) boneless, skinless chicken thighs or breasts, cut into bite-size pieces

1 lb (450 g) asparagus, cut into 1-inch (3-cm) pieces

2 cups (320 g) cherry tomatoes

2 green onions, thinly sliced

½ cup (85 g) diced yellow bell pepper

DIRECTIONS

To make the Lemon-Dijon Dressing, combine the lemon juice, mustard, oil, honey, rosemary and pepper to a small cruet or lidded container. Shake well to combine.

To make the salad, cook the rotini according to the package directions so that it is al dente. Drain the rotini, rinse it and set it aside.

Heat the oil in a large skillet over medium-high heat. Add the chicken and cook until the meat is browned on all sides, approximately 5 minutes. Reduce the heat to medium. Add the asparagus and cook until the asparagus is fork-tender and the chicken is cooked through and the juices run clear, approximately 6 to 8 minutes. Remove the skillet from the heat and let the mixture sit for 5 minutes.

Add the rotini, tomatoes, green onions and bell pepper to a large bowl. Add the chicken and asparagus. Toss to combine. Drizzle the dressing over the pasta salad. Toss to coat.

STORING

Either cover and store the salad in the large bowl or divide the salad between 8 lidded containers. Store in the refrigerator for up to 5 days.

GREEK STEAK AND LENTIL SALAD

The Greek Dressing makes this salad satisfyingly flavorful. And the combination of steak and lentils makes this a hearty, nutrient-dense meal. It is delicious served warm or cold, though I prefer it cold.

GREEK DRESSING

6 tbsp (90 g) red wine vinegar

4 tbsp + 2 tsp (70 ml) olive oil

1½ tsp (2 g) dried oregano

1½ tsp (2 g) dried basil

1½ tsp (5 g) garlic powder

¾ tsp Dijon mustard

¾ tsp onion powder

¼ tsp Seasoned Salt (page 191)

⅛ tsp coarsely ground pepper

SALAD

1 lb (450 g) steak, cut into bite-size pieces

½ cup (68 g) diced red onion

2 medium ribs celery, thinly sliced

1 pint (322 g) cherry tomatoes

1 cup (180 g) sliced black olives

3 cups (603 g) cooked lentils

DIRECTIONS

To make the Greek Dressing, combine the vinegar, oil, oregano, basil, garlic powder, mustard, onion powder, Seasoned Salt and pepper in a medium cruet or lidded jar. Shake well to mix.

To make the salad, add 2 tablespoons (30 ml) of Greek Dressing and the steak to a medium skillet over medium heat. Cook until the steak is cooked through, approximately 6 to 8 minutes.

Add the onion, celery, tomatoes and olives to a large bowl. Add the cooked steak and lentils. Toss to thoroughly combine. Drizzle the dressing over the salad. Toss to coat.

STORING

Either cover and store the salad in the large bowl or divide the salad between 4 lidded containers. Store in the refrigerator for up to 5 days.

ASIAN CHICKEN QUINOA SALAD

I have never met an Asian chicken salad that I haven't liked. However, I don't like how the crispy noodles and salad greens get soggy when packed in a lunch. I decided to substitute cabbage for the lettuce. And I chose to leave the noodles out and replace them with quinoa. Quinoa has a little nutty crunch to it that blends well with the flavors in Asian chicken salad.

DRESSING

¼ cup (60 ml) rice vinegar

¼ cup (60 ml) soy sauce

⅓ cup (80 ml) mild-tasting oil

1 tbsp (15 ml) sesame oil

2 tbsp (30 ml) honey

2 tbsp (29 g) grated fresh ginger

½ tsp garlic powder

SALAD

1 lb (450 g) boneless, skinless chicken thighs or breasts, cut into bite-size pieces

3 cups (1 kg) thinly sliced cabbage

1 cup (341 g) julienned carrots

½ cup (68 g) diced onion

1 medium red bell pepper, diced

6 oz (168 g) snow peas

1 cup (270 g) fresh bean sprouts

3 cups (483 g) cooked quinoa (page 90)

2 tbsp (20 g) sesame seeds

DIRECTIONS

To make the dressing, add the vinegar, soy sauce, mild-tasting oil, sesame oil, honey, ginger and garlic powder to a medium cruet or lidded jar. Shake vigorously to combine.

To make the salad, add 2 tablespoons (30 ml) of dressing and the chicken to a medium skillet over medium heat. Cook until the chicken is cooked through, approximately 10 minutes.

In a large bowl, combine the cabbage, carrots, onion, bell pepper, snow peas, bean sprouts and quinoa. Toss to thoroughly combine.

Pour the dressing over the salad and toss to thoroughly coat. Refrigerate for approximately 2 hours before serving.

STORING

Either cover and store the salad in the large bowl or divide the salad between 6 lidded containers. Store in the refrigerator for up to 5 days.

CATALINA CHICKEN
TACO PASTA SALAD

The dressing on this salad combines the sweetness of Catalina dressing with the bite of taco spices. The sweetness offsets the heat, making it perfect for those who prefer mildly spicy Southwestern dishes.

DRESSING

Juice and zest of 1 lime

3 tbsp (45 ml) olive oil

3 tbsp (45 ml) water

3 tbsp (45 ml) honey

3 tbsp (45 ml) tomato sauce

2 tbsp (18 g) Taco Seasoning Mix (page 190)

SALAD

12 oz (340 g) rotini pasta

1 tbsp (15 ml) olive oil

1 lb (450 g) boneless, skinless chicken thighs or breasts, cut into bite-size pieces

1 tbsp (9 g) Taco Seasoning Mix (page 190)

2 cups (320 g) cherry tomatoes

1¾ cups (253 g) corn or 1 (15-oz [424-g]) can corn, drained

1¾ cups (351 g) cooked black beans or 1 (15-oz [424-g]) can black beans, drained and rinsed

⅓ cup (45 g) diced red onion

1 medium rib celery, thinly sliced

DIRECTIONS

To make the dressing, combine the lime juice and zest, oil, water, honey, tomato sauce and Taco Seasoning Mix in a small cruet or lidded jar. Shake well to mix.

To make the salad, cook the rotini according to the package directions. Drain the rotini, rinse it and set it aside.

Heat the oil in a medium skillet over medium-high heat. Add the chicken and Taco Seasoning Mix. Toss to coat. Cook until the chicken is cooked through, approximately 6 to 8 minutes.

Add the rotini to a large bowl. Add the chicken, tomatoes, corn, black beans, onion and celery. Toss to mix. Drizzle the dressing over the pasta salad. Toss to coat.

Cover the pasta salad and chill for 2 hours before serving.

STORING

Either store the salad in the large bowl or divide the salad between 6 lidded containers. Store in the refrigerator for up to 5 days.

PIZZA QUINOA SALAD

This has all of your favorite pizza toppings mixed with hearty quinoa and drizzled with a Zesty Italian Dressing. It is a healthier option to satisfy your pizza cravings. If you already have some cooked quinoa on hand, this salad will come together in minutes.

ZESTY ITALIAN DRESSING

⅓ cup (80 ml) olive oil

¼ cup (60 ml) balsamic vinegar

1 tbsp (15 ml) water

1½ tsp (6 g) sugar

¾ tsp dried oregano

½ tsp garlic powder

½ tsp onion powder

¼ tsp dried thyme

¼ tsp dried basil

¼ tsp red pepper flakes

⅛ tsp coarsely ground pepper

SALAD

3 cups (483 g) cooked quinoa (pages 90)

2 cups (320 g) cherry tomatoes, quartered

1 cup (130 g) shredded mozzarella cheese

½ cup (60 g) shredded mild cheddar cheese

1 medium green bell pepper, diced

½ cup (68 g) diced red onion

1 (3.8-oz [106-g]) can sliced black olives, drained

1 cup (66 g) sliced mushrooms

1 cup (230 g) mini pepperoni slices

DIRECTIONS

To make the Zesty Italian Dressing, combine the oil, vinegar, water, sugar, oregano, garlic powder, onion powder, thyme, basil, red pepper flakes and pepper in a small cruet or lidded jar. Shake well to mix.

To make the salad, add the quinoa, tomatoes, mozzarella, cheddar, bell pepper, onion, olives, mushrooms and pepperoni to a large bowl. Stir to combine. Drizzle the dressing over the salad. Toss to coat.

STORING

Either cover and store the salad in the large bowl or divide the salad between 5 lidded containers. Store in the refrigerator for up to 5 days.

SALAD BAR VEGETABLE SALAD

When my daughter goes to a salad bar, she loads her plate up with just about every vegetable available except for the lettuces and salad greens. Not only does this salad have all of my daughter's favorite veggies, it is a sturdy salad that holds up well during travel.

CREAMY BALSAMIC DRESSING

3 tbsp (45 ml) olive oil

3 tbsp (45 ml) balsamic vinegar

3 tbsp (45 ml) mayonnaise

2 tbsp (30 ml) water

1 tsp Dijon mustard

1 tsp sugar

¼ tsp garlic powder

¼ tsp dried oregano

SALAD

2 cups (682 g) julienned broccoli stems

1 cup (151 g) snap peas

1 cup (341 g) shredded carrots

1 cup (66 g) sliced baby portobello mushrooms

1 cup (170 g) sliced celery

½ cup (85 g) diced red bell pepper

¼ cup (34 g) diced red onion

1 (15-oz [424-g]) can corn, drained

1¾ cups (351 g) cooked garbanzo beans or 1 (15-oz [424-g]) can garbanzo beans, drained and rinsed

DIRECTIONS

To make the Creamy Balsamic Dressing, combine the oil, vinegar, mayonnaise, water, mustard, sugar, garlic powder and oregano in a medium cruet or lidded jar. Shake well to mix.

To make the salad, combine the broccoli stems, snap peas, carrots, mushrooms, celery, bell pepper, onion, corn and beans in a large bowl. Pour the dressing over the vegetables. Stir until the vegetables are completely coated.

STORING

Either cover and store the salad in the large bowl or divide the salad between 5 lidded containers. Store in the refrigerator for up to 5 days.

CHOPPED BARBECUE PORK SALAD

This tastes like a Sunday barbecue rolled up into a salad. Since the pork chops are broiled, this salad comes together fast.

INGREDIENTS

1 lb (450 g) boneless pork chops

½ cup (120 ml) Barbecue Sauce (page 196), divided

6 cups (216 g) chopped kale

2 cups (320 g) cherry tomatoes

1 (15-oz [424-g]) can corn, drained

1 cup (170 g) diced red or orange bell pepper

4 green onions, thinly sliced

1 cup (120 g) shredded medium cheddar cheese

½ cup (120 ml) Ranch Salad Dressing (page 194)

DIRECTIONS

Preheat the oven to broil and set the rack 6 inches (15 cm) below the heat source. Line a medium baking sheet with foil.

Place the pork chops on the baking sheet. Place ¼ cup (60 ml) of the Barbecue Sauce in a small bowl. Brush the exposed sides of the pork chops with the Barbecue Sauce. Broil for 8 to 12 minutes. Flip the pork chops over and brush the other sides with the Barbecue Sauce. Broil for 8 to 12 minutes, or until the juices run clear and the meat has reached an internal temperature of 145°F (63°C). Let the pork chops rest for 5 minutes. Cut them into bite-size pieces.

Add the kale, tomatoes, corn, bell pepper, green onions and cheddar to a large bowl. Add the pork. Toss to combine. Drizzle with the Ranch Salad Dressing and the remaining ¼ cup (60 ml) of Barbecue Sauce over the salad. Toss to coat.

STORING
Either cover and store the salad in the large bowl or divide the salad between 6 lidded containers. Store in the refrigerator for up to 5 days.

Chapter 6

MUST-HAVE SANDWICHES, WRAPS AND MORE

Sandwiches are a lunch staple because they are easy to eat on the go. However, it's easy for us to fall into a rut by making the same sandwich each day. In this chapter, you will find new sandwich ideas to add variety to your lunches.

TIPS FOR PREVENTING SOGGY BREAD

No one likes a sandwich with soggy bread! There are several ways you can prevent your bread from absorbing liquid from your sandwich fillings and becoming soggy.

Choose your bread wisely when making a sandwich. Skip the white sandwich bread, and choose sturdier, denser, crustier breads for your sandwiches, such as rolls, bagels, English muffins and whole-grain breads.

If you choose to use sandwich bread, toast it before making your sandwich. This will make the bread drier, so it won't become soggy if it absorbs some of the moisture from your sandwich fillings.

You can apply a thin layer of butter to your bread before building your sandwich. The butter acts as a barrier to prevent the bread from absorbing the liquids. Depending on the flavor profile of the sandwich, you could substitute softened cream cheese or ricotta cheese for the butter.

Add a large lettuce leaf or a slice of cheese next to the bread to prevent any moisture from the other ingredients from being absorbed by the bread.

Apply condiments to the center of your sandwich—between the meat and lettuce—to prevent the condiments from soaking into the bread.

Make sure your lettuce and other greens are dry before adding them to your sandwich. Place juicy vegetables (such as tomatoes and pickles) in the center of your sandwich rather than next to the bread.

FRENCH DIP GRILLED CHEESE SANDWICH

This comes together quickly if you choose not to caramelize the onions. But it is worth the wait to caramelize the onions! Serve this with the Au Jus (below).

INGREDIENTS

1 tbsp (15 ml) olive oil

1 tbsp (15 ml) balsamic vinegar

1 large yellow onion, thinly sliced

¼ cup (60 ml) mayonnaise

1 tbsp (15 ml) horseradish

1 tbsp (15 g) butter

1 large loaf crusty French bread, cut into 16 (½-inch [13-mm] thick) slices

16 slices provolone cheese

1 lb (450 g) thinly sliced roast beef

DIRECTIONS

Heat the oil and vinegar in a large skillet over medium heat. Add the onion and stir gently to coat the onion slices with the oil and vinegar. Check the onion every 5 minutes. Stir the onion and scrape up the fond (i.e., the browned bits of food) that forms on the bottom of the skillet. Cook the onion until it develops a deep brown color, 20 to 30 minutes.

In a small bowl, combine the mayonnaise and horseradish.

Add the butter to a large skillet over medium-high heat. Place 2 pieces of bread in the skillet for each sandwich. Place a slice of provolone on each piece of bread. Place 2 ounces (56 g) of roast beef on 1 of the slices of bread. Drizzle a little of the horseradish mayonnaise on the meat. Spoon some caramelized onion on top of the horseradish mayonnaise. Place the piece of bread with only the provolone on top of the dressed onion. Cook until the bottom slice of bread is golden brown, about 3 to 4 minutes. Flip and cook until the other slice is golden brown, about 3 to 4 minutes. Repeat this process until all of the sandwiches have been made.

STORING AND REHEATING

Allow the sandwiches to cool before storing. Place them in an airtight container and store in the refrigerator for up to 3 days.

To freeze, wrap each sandwich individually and freeze for up to 1 month.

To reheat a thawed sandwich, unwrap it, place it on a microwave-safe plate and microwave on high for 30 to 45 seconds.

To reheat a frozen sandwich, unwrap it, place it on a microwave-safe plate and microwave it at 50 percent power for 3 minutes.

QUICK AND EASY AU JUS

INGREDIENTS

1½ cups (360 ml) water

2 beef bouillon cubes

¼ tsp garlic powder

¼ tsp onion powder

½ tsp soy sauce

2 tsp (6 g) cornstarch (optional)

Pinch of Seasoned Salt (page 191)

Dash of coarsely ground pepper

DIRECTIONS

In a medium saucepan over medium-high heat, combine the water, bouillon cubes, garlic powder, onion powder, soy sauce, cornstarch, Seasoned Salt and pepper. Cook until the mixture reaches a boil. Reduce the heat to low and simmer for 10 minutes.

TERIYAKI SLIDERS

Makes 12

These sliders are an Asian-inspired alternative to the traditional game day sliders. Both the meat and the slaw in these sliders have a rich flavor, so you don't need to add any additional condiments to the burgers.

TERIYAKI BURGERS

2 lb (900 g) ground beef

¼ cup (60 ml) teriyaki sauce

1 tsp honey

1 tsp sesame oil, optional

1 tsp onion powder

½ tsp garlic powder

½ tsp ground ginger

ASIAN BROCCOLI SLAW

2½ cups (853 g) julienned broccoli stems

¼ cup (85 g) shredded purple cabbage

¼ cup (85 g) julienned carrots

1 tbsp (15 ml) mild-tasting oil

2 tsp (10 ml) rice vinegar

2 tsp (10 ml) soy sauce

2 tsp (10 ml) honey

1 tsp sesame oil

¼ tsp ground ginger

¼ tsp garlic powder

SLIDERS

12 Hawaiian-style rolls

1 tbsp (15 ml) mild-tasting oil

1½ tsp (5 g) sesame seeds

DIRECTIONS

Preheat the oven to 350°F (177°C). Grease a 9 x 12-inch (23 x 30-cm) baking pan, then line it with parchment paper.

In a medium bowl, combine the ground beef with the teriyaki sauce, honey, sesame oil if desired, onion powder, garlic powder and ground ginger. Mix well until the spices are fully incorporated.

Press the ground beef mixture into the baking pan.

Bake the beef for 20 minutes, or until the meat is cooked through.

While the meat is cooking, make the broccoli slaw by combining the broccoli, cabbage and carrots in a medium bowl. Add the oil, vinegar, soy sauce, honey, sesame oil, ginger and garlic powder to a cruet or lidded jar. Shake well to blend. Pour the dressing over the broccoli slaw and toss to coat well.

When the meat is done cooking, remove it from the oven and brush any oil from the top with a pastry brush or blot it with a paper towel. Do not turn off the oven.

To make the sliders, cut the rolls in half and place the bottom halves of the rolls in a 12 x 9-inch (30 x 23-cm) casserole dish. Place the meat on top of the rolls. Spread the broccoli slaw over the meat. Place the top halves of the rolls over the sandwiches. Baste the tops of the rolls with the oil and sprinkle the sesame seeds over them.

Cover the casserole dish with foil and bake for 15 minutes, or until the sandwiches are heated through.

Cut the sliders along the lines of the rolls and serve.

STORING AND REHEATING

Allow the sliders to cool before storing. Place them in an airtight container and store in the refrigerator for up to 3 days.

To freeze, wrap each slider individually and freeze for up to 1 month.

To reheat a thawed slider, unwrap it, place it on a microwave-safe plate and microwave on high for 20 to 30 seconds.

To reheat a frozen slider, unwrap it, place it on a microwave-safe plate and microwave it at 50 percent power for 2 to 2½ minutes.

Makes
6

CHICKEN MARSALA POCKET

These tasty pocket sandwiches are easy to make. They rely on frozen puff pastry to create a tender and flaky crust. Although they look a little plain on the outside, the chicken marsala provides a powerful punch of flavor.

INGREDIENTS

2 tbsp (20 g) cornstarch

¼ tsp Seasoned Salt (page 191)

Dash of coarsely ground pepper

1 tbsp (14 g) butter, melted

1 lb (450 g) boneless, skinless chicken thighs or breasts, cut into bite-size pieces

1 tbsp (15 ml) olive oil

¼ cup (60 ml) Marsala wine

2 tbsp (30 ml) milk

½ tsp garlic powder

½ tsp onion powder

1½ cups (99 g) sliced mushrooms

2 sheets puff pastry

DIRECTIONS

Preheat the oven to 425°F (218°C). Line a 9 x 13-inch (23 x 33-cm) baking sheet with parchment paper.

Combine the cornstarch, Seasoned Salt and pepper in large sealable plastic bag. Place the butter in a pie pan or shallow bowl. Dip the chicken pieces in the melted butter; place the chicken pieces in the bag. Seal the bag tightly and shake to coat the chicken.

Heat the oil in a large skillet over medium-high heat. Add the chicken and cook for 6 to 8 minutes, or until the chicken is browned, turning once during the cooking time. Add the Marsala, milk, garlic powder, onion powder and mushrooms. Cook 4 to 6 minutes, or until the chicken is no longer pink and the sauce is slightly thickened.

Unwrap 1 sheet of puff pastry on a large cutting board. Use a dusted rolling pin to roll the puff pastry out a bit and flatten the seams. Using a pizza cutter or knife, cut the pastry lengthwise into 3 equal strips. Cut each strip in half crosswise for a total of 6 equal rectangles. Transfer the rectangles to the baking sheet and repeat this process with the other pastry sheet.

Divide the chicken mixture between 6 of the puff pastry rectangles. Brush the exposed pastry with a wet basting brush. Top the chicken mixture with the other 6 puff pastry rectangles. Use a fork to press each pocket closed.

Bake for 15 to 20 minutes, or until the pockets are golden brown and flaky.

STORING AND REHEATING

Allow the pockets to cool before storing. Place them in an airtight container and store in the refrigerator for up to 3 days.

To freeze, wrap each pocket individually and freeze for up to 1 month.

To reheat a thawed pocket, unwrap it, place it on a microwave-safe plate and microwave on high for 30 seconds.

To reheat a frozen pocket, unwrap it, place it on a microwave-safe plate and microwave it at 50 percent power for 2 minutes.

JALAPEÑO CHICKEN PITA POCKETS

This hearty pita pocket has a bold jalapeño flavor, but since the peppers are deseeded, it is not too spicy.

INGREDIENTS

1 tbsp (15 ml) olive oil

1½ lb (675 g) boneless, skinless chicken thighs or breasts, cut into bite-size pieces

2 medium jalapeño peppers, deseeded and diced

2 green onions, thinly sliced

¾ cup (90 g) shredded cheddar cheese

¾ cup (98 g) shredded Monterey Jack cheese

3 pitas, cut in half

DIRECTIONS

Heat the oil in a large skillet over medium-high heat. Place the chicken in the skillet and cook until the chicken is cooked through, approximately 10 minutes.

Remove the skillet from the heat. Drain any excess chicken fat from the skillet. Add the jalapeños, green onions, cheddar and Monterey Jack. Stir until the ingredients are just combined.

Divide the chicken mixture between the pita pockets.

STORING AND REHEATING

Allow the pockets to cool before storing. Place them in an airtight container and store in the refrigerator for up to 3 days.

To freeze, wrap each pocket individually and freeze for up to 1 month.

To reheat a thawed pocket, unwrap it, place it on a microwave-safe plate and microwave on high for 30 to 45 seconds.

To reheat a frozen pocket, unwrap it, place it on a microwave-safe plate and microwave it at 50 percent power for 3 minutes.

Makes 6

HONEY MUSTARD HAM AND CHEESE QUESADILLAS WITH BROCCOLI

I always make use of as much of each vegetable as I can. When I use broccoli florets for one dish, I save the stems to julienne and use in another dish. I actually prefer broccoli stems to florets, because they hold up better under heat.

INGREDIENTS

3 tbsp (45 ml) honey

3 tbsp (45 ml) yellow mustard

1 tbsp (15 ml) mild-tasting oil

12 (6-inch [15-cm]) tortillas

¾ cup (90 g) shredded cheddar cheese

¾ cup (98 g) shredded mozzarella cheese

1 lb (450 g) thinly sliced ham

1½ cups (512 g) julienned broccoli stems

1 green onion, thinly sliced

DIRECTIONS

In a small bowl, combine the honey and mustard.

Heat the oil in a large skillet over medium-high heat. Place a tortilla in the skillet. Place 1 tablespoon (8 g) of cheddar and 1 tablespoon (8 g) of mozzarella on the tortilla. Place several slices of ham on the cheeses. Spoon some honey mustard on top of the ham. Add ¼ cup (85 g) of broccoli and some green onion to the ham. Add 1 tablespoon (8 g) of cheddar and 1 tablespoon (8 g) of mozzarella and place another tortilla on top. Cook until the bottom tortilla is golden brown, about 3 to 4 minutes. Flip and cook until the other side is golden brown, about 3 to 4 minutes. Repeat this process until all of the quesadillas have been made.

STORING AND REHEATING

Allow the quesadillas to cool before storing. Place them in an airtight container and store in the refrigerator for up to 3 days.

To freeze, place parchment paper between the quesadillas and freeze for up to 1 month.

To reheat a thawed quesadilla, unwrap it, place it on a microwave-safe plate and microwave on high for 30 to 45 seconds.

To reheat a frozen quesadilla, unwrap it, place it on a microwave-safe plate and microwave it at 50 percent power for 2 minutes.

TUSCAN PORK
QUESADILLA

Whenever I ask my husband what kind of cheese I should use in a dish he says, "Provolone." It doesn't matter what I am making—he always requests provolone cheese. I usually explain why provolone isn't a good match for what I am making, but when he suggested I use it in these Tuscan Pork Quesadillas, I knew he was on to something.

INGREDIENTS

1 tbsp (15 ml) olive oil, plus more as needed

¾ lb (338 g) pork, cut into bite-size pieces

2 tsp (2 g) dried oregano

1 tsp dried basil

1 tsp garlic powder

1 tsp onion powder

12 (6-inch [15-cm]) tortillas

12 slices provolone cheese

18 slices Roma tomato

DIRECTIONS

Heat the oil in a large skillet over medium-high heat. Add the pork and sauté until the pork is browned on all sides, approximately 5 minutes. Add the oregano, basil, garlic powder and onion power. Toss to coat. Cook until the pork is cooked through, approximately 5 minutes. Transfer the pork to a medium bowl and return the skillet to the heat.

Add 1 tablespoon (15 ml) of oil to the skillet. Place 1 tortilla in the skillet. Place a slice of provolone on the tortilla. Place 3 slices of tomato on the provolone. Spoon some Tuscan pork on top of the tomatoes. Place another slice of provolone on top of the pork and then place another tortilla on top. Cook until the bottom tortilla is golden brown, about 3 to 4 minutes. Flip and cook until the other tortilla is golden brown, about 3 to 4 minutes. Repeat this process until all of the quesadillas have been made.

STORING AND REHEATING

Allow the quesadillas to cool before storing. Place them in an airtight container and store in the refrigerator for up to 3 days.

To freeze, place parchment paper between the quesadillas and freeze for up to 1 month.

To reheat a thawed quesadilla, unwrap it, place it on a microwave-safe plate and microwave on high for 30 to 45 seconds.

To reheat a frozen quesadilla, unwrap it, place it on a microwave-safe plate and microwave it at 50 percent power for 2 minutes.

Serves 8

SOUTHWESTERN CHICKEN SALAD LETTUCE WRAP

This is a flavorful twist on traditional chicken salad recipes. I serve this on lettuce, but you can use a tortilla if you prefer.

INGREDIENTS

1 lb (450 g) boneless, skinless chicken breasts or thighs

2 medium Roma tomatoes, diced

½ cup (68 g) diced onion

1 medium green bell pepper, diced

¼ cup (10 g) fresh cilantro, chopped

⅓ cup (80 ml) tomato juice

2 cloves garlic, minced

1 tsp ground cumin

½ tsp dried marjoram

8 large romaine lettuce leaves

¼ cup (33 g) shredded Monterey Jack cheese

¼ cup (30 g) shredded medium cheddar cheese

DIRECTIONS

Preheat the oven to broil. Set the rack 6 inches (15 cm) below the heat source. Cover a broiler pan with foil.

Broil the chicken breasts for 4 to 6 minutes. Flip the chicken breasts and broil for 4 to 6 minutes, or until the juices run clear and the chicken reaches an internal temperature of 165°F (74°C). Remove the chicken from the oven and let it sit for 5 minutes. Cut the chicken into bite-size pieces.

In a medium bowl, combine the chicken, tomatoes, onion, bell pepper and cilantro.

In a small bowl, combine the tomato juice, garlic, cumin and marjoram. Mix well. Pour the juice mixture over the chicken and vegetables. Stir well.

Divide the chicken salad between the romaine lettuce leaves. Sprinkle the Monterey Jack and cheddar over the top of the salad.

STORING
Store the chicken salad in an airtight container in the refrigerator for up to 3 days.

Makes 6

RATATOUILLE GRILLED CHEESE SANDWICH

This recipe began as a way to use up leftover ratatouille, but it was so popular with my family that I started making a small batch of ratatouille just to make these grilled cheese sandwiches.

INGREDIENTS

¼ cup (34 g) diced red onion

6 tbsp (90 ml) Italian Dressing (page 193), divided

¼ cup (43 g) diced green bell pepper

1 cup (201 g) diced eggplant

½ cup (38 g) diced zucchini

½ cup (38 g) diced yellow squash

½ cup (80 g) diced Roma tomatoes

¼ cup (19 g) diced baby portobello mushrooms

12 slices sandwich bread

12 slices medium cheddar cheese

DIRECTIONS

Add the onion and 1 tablespoon (15 ml) of the Italian Dressing to a large skillet over medium-high heat. Sauté until the onion is tender, approximately 3 minutes.

Add the bell pepper, eggplant, zucchini, yellow squash, tomatoes and mushrooms to the skillet. Drizzle 3 tablespoons (45 ml) of the Italian Dressing over the vegetables. Cook over medium heat until the vegetables are fork-tender, approximately 10 minutes.

Transfer the vegetables to a medium bowl and set aside.

Add 1 tablespoon (15 ml) of the Italian Dressing to the skillet. Place 6 pieces of bread in the skillet. Place a slice of cheddar on each piece of bread. Spoon the ratatouille onto 3 slices of bread. Flip the pieces of bread with just cheese on top of the ratatouille. Cook until the bottom slices are golden brown, about 3 to 4 minutes. Flip and cook until the other slice is golden brown, about 3 to 4 minutes. Add a tablespoon (15 ml) of Italian Dressing and repeat until all of the sandwiches have been made.

STORING AND REHEATING

Allow the sandwiches to cool before storing. Place them in an airtight container and store in the refrigerator for up to 3 days.

To freeze, wrap each sandwich individually and freeze for up to 1 month.

To reheat a thawed sandwich, unwrap it, place it on a microwave-safe plate and microwave on high for 30 to 45 seconds.

To reheat a frozen sandwich, unwrap it, place it on a microwave-safe plate and microwave it at 50 percent power for 3 minutes.

Chapter 7

EASY SOUPS, STEWS AND CHILIS

Soups, stews and chilis are perfect make-ahead lunches. They keep well in the refrigerator and can be frozen for months. When making soups ahead of time for lunches, you want to avoid rice and pasta as they continue to absorb the liquid in the soup. If you like rice in your soups, cauliflower rice makes a good substitute for the grain in make-ahead soups. Replace the amount of cooked rice you would normally add to a soup with an equal amount of raw cauliflower rice.

TIPS FOR FREEZING INDIVIDUAL SERVINGS OF SOUP, STEW AND CHILI

Allow the soup, stew or chili to cool off before freezing.

Put the soup in a freezer-safe dish, preferably one that is also microwave-safe. I prefer to use tempered glass containers with tight-fitting lids.

Allow room for expansion. The broth will expand as it freezes. Leave room in the container to allow for that.

I like to freeze my soups but I don't want to keep dozens of containers tied up in the freezer. My trick? Line the containers with clear plastic wrap and leave several inches hanging over the sides of the container. Add the soup and let it freeze. Once it is frozen solid, remove it from the container. Use the excess plastic to cover the top. Then place the individually wrapped frozen soups in a sealable freezer bag. When you want to place a soup in a lunch, remove a serving from the bag, unwrap it and then place it inside the container it was frozen in. Place a lid on the container and put it in the refrigerator to thaw overnight.

It is always best to thaw frozen soup in the refrigerator overnight. If that isn't possible, place the frozen container in a pan of cold water on the counter. It should thaw within 30 to 60 minutes. I have included instructions for thawing and reheating frozen soups in the microwave, although this method should always be a last resort.

TACO CAULIFLOWER-RICE SOUP

My family enjoys taco rice soup, but as it sits in the refrigerator for a day or two, the rice absorbs the liquid. I have found a way to work around that problem by using cauliflower rice instead.

INGREDIENTS

1 lb (450 g) ground beef

1 cup (135 g) diced onion

½ cup (85 g) diced green bell pepper

1¾ cups (351 g) cooked black beans or 1 (15-oz [424-g]) can black beans, drained and rinsed

2 cups (421 g) cauliflower rice (page 87)

3½ cups (563 g) fresh diced tomatoes or 2 (15-oz [424-g]) cans diced tomatoes, undrained

1 (15-oz [450-ml]) can tomato sauce

3 tbsp (27 g) Taco Seasoning Mix (page 190)

1 cup (240 ml) water

¾ cup (90 g) shredded Monterey Jack cheese

¾ cup (90 g) shredded cheddar cheese

6 cups (750 g) tortilla chips (optional)

DIRECTIONS

In a large pot, combine the ground beef, onion and bell pepper over medium-high heat. Cook until the ground beef is browned and cooked through, approximately 5 minutes.

Add the beans, cauliflower rice, diced tomatoes, tomato sauce, Taco Seasoning Mix and water. Bring the soup to a boil. Reduce the heat to low and simmer for 10 minutes.

Top each bowl of soup with 2 tablespoons (30 g) of Monterey Jack cheese and 2 tablespoons (30 g) of cheddar cheese. Serve with tortilla chips.

STORING AND REHEATING

Place the soup in a large covered bowl or individual containers. Store in the refrigerator for up to 5 days or in the freezer for 3 months.

To freeze, ensure the soup has cooled completely then place it in freezer-safe containers. Leave room in the containers for the liquid to expand. If possible, thaw the soup overnight in the refrigerator.

To reheat the thawed soup, place it in a microwave-safe dish and microwave on high for 40 to 60 seconds.

To reheat a frozen bowl of soup, first ensure the container is microwave-safe. Remove the lid and cover the container with a paper towel. Microwave it at 50 percent power for 3 minutes. Continue adding 1 minute at a time until you can stir the soup. Stir the soup to see if it is heated all the way through. If not, microwave on high for 30 to 40 seconds.

CARROT SOUP
WITH LENTILS

I enjoy carrot gazpacho, but since it is a raw soup, I don't feel comfortable keeping it in the fridge too long. This carrot soup has the flavors of my favorite gazpacho, but I can safely keep it in the refrigerator for 5 days. I include red lentils to add a little extra protein.

INGREDIENTS

1 tbsp (15 ml) olive oil

1 cup (135 g) diced onion

1 medium rib celery, finely chopped

2 lb (900 g) carrots, finely chopped

4 cloves garlic, minced

8 cups (1.9 L) vegetable broth

½ cup (101 g) uncooked red lentils

1 tsp ground turmeric

2 tsp (6 g) ground ginger

½ tsp red pepper flakes

DIRECTIONS

Heat the oil in a large pot over medium-high heat. Add the onion, celery and carrots. Sauté for 5 minutes, or until the onion is translucent. Add the garlic and sauté for 1 minute.

Add the broth, lentils, turmeric, ginger and red pepper flakes. Stir to combine. Bring the soup to a boil. Put a lid on the pot, reduce the heat to low and simmer for 20 minutes, or until the carrots are very tender and the lentils can be smashed with a spoon.

Remove the soup from the heat. Use an immersion blender to puree the soup or carefully ladle the soup into a conventional blender to puree it. (If you use a conventional blender, it may be safer to do this in batches. After you put the lid on the blender, put a kitchen towel on top of the lid and hold the lid down while blending to prevent hot soup from splashing you.) Return the soup to the pot. Simmer for 10 minutes.

STORING AND REHEATING

Place the soup in a large covered bowl or individual containers. Store in the refrigerator for up to 5 days or in the freezer for 3 months.

To freeze, ensure the soup has cooled completely then place it in freezer-safe containers. Leave room in the containers for the liquid to expand. If possible, thaw the frozen soup overnight in the refrigerator.

To reheat the thawed soup, place it in a microwave-safe dish and microwave on high for 40 to 60 seconds.

To reheat a frozen bowl of soup, first ensure the container is microwave-safe. Remove the lid and cover the container with a paper towel. Microwave it at 50 percent power for 3 minutes. Continue adding 1 minute at a time until you can stir the soup. Stir the soup to see if it is heated all the way through. If not, microwave on high for 20 to 30 seconds to heat it through.

HEARTY STEAK AND MUSHROOM STEW

This hearty stew combines the flavors of mushroom soup and beef stew. It comes together quickly and keeps well.

INGREDIENTS

1 tbsp (15 ml) olive oil

1 lb (450 g) steak, cut into bite-size pieces

¾ cup (102 g) diced onion

2 medium ribs celery, thinly sliced

4 cloves garlic, minced

6 red potatoes, diced

1 cup (152 g) thinly sliced carrots

8 oz (224 g) sliced mushrooms

2 tbsp (20 g) cornstarch

4 cups (960 ml) beef broth, divided

1 tsp dried rosemary

½ tsp Seasoned Salt (page 191)

¼ tsp coarsely ground pepper

DIRECTIONS

Heat the olive oil in a large pot over medium-high heat. Add the steak, onion and celery. Sauté for 5 minutes, or until the steak is browned on all sides.

Add the garlic, potatoes and carrots to the steak and sauté for 5 minutes. Add the mushrooms and sauté for 3 minutes.

Place the cornstarch in a small bowl. Slowly whisk 1 cup (240 ml) of the broth into the cornstarch until the cornstarch is completely incorporated into the broth and the mixture is free of lumps. Add this mixture to the steak and vegetables.

Add the remaining 3 cups (720 ml) of broth, rosemary, Seasoned Salt and pepper. Stir until thoroughly combined. Bring the stew to a boil. Reduce the heat to low and simmer for 10 minutes.

STORING AND REHEATING

Place the stew in a large covered bowl or individual containers. Store in the refrigerator for up to 5 days or in the freezer for 3 months.

To freeze, ensure the stew has cooled completely then place it in freezer-safe containers. Leave room in the containers for the liquid to expand. If possible, thaw the frozen stew overnight in the refrigerator.

To reheat the thawed stew, place it in a microwave-safe dish and microwave on high for 40 to 60 seconds.

To reheat a frozen bowl of stew, first ensure the container is microwave-safe. Remove the lid and cover the container with a paper towel. Microwave it at 50 percent power for 3 minutes, or until you can stir it. Microwave on high for 40 seconds, or until it is heated through.

BUFFALO RANCH CHICKEN SOUP

All I have to say is "Buffalo ranch chicken," and my family comes running. Unfortunately, many Buffalo ranch chicken recipes are loaded with fat. I decided to create a guilt-free version my family could enjoy any day of the week.

INGREDIENTS

1 tbsp (15 ml) olive oil

1 lb (450 g) boneless, skinless chicken thighs or breasts, cut into bite-size pieces

1 cup (135 g) diced onion

½ cup (85 g) diced green bell pepper

2 medium ribs celery, thinly sliced

4 cloves garlic, minced

1 tsp dried parsley

1 tsp dried thyme

1 tsp Seasoned Salt (page 191)

¼ tsp coarsely ground pepper

2 cups (480 ml) chicken broth

3½ cups (704 g) cooked cannellini beans or 2 (15-oz [424-g]) cans cannellini beans, drained and rinsed

1¾ cups (282 g) fresh diced tomatoes or 1 (15-oz [424-g]) can diced tomatoes, undrained

¼ cup (60 ml) hot sauce

½ cup (123 g) plain yogurt

½ cup (62 g) ricotta cheese, softened

DIRECTIONS

Heat the oil in a large pot over medium-high heat. Add the chicken, onion, bell pepper and celery. Sauté for 5 minutes, or until the chicken is browned on all sides.

Add the garlic, parsley, thyme, Seasoned Salt and pepper to the chicken. Toss to coat and sauté for 1 minute.

Add the broth, beans, diced tomatoes and hot sauce. Stir to thoroughly combine. Cook until the soup reaches a boil. Reduce the heat to low and simmer for 10 minutes. Remove from the heat.

Stir in the yogurt and ricotta until the ricotta is fully melted and incorporated into the broth.

STORING AND REHEATING

Place the soup in a large covered bowl or individual containers. Store in the refrigerator for up to 5 days or in the freezer for 3 months.

To freeze, ensure the soup has cooled completely then place it in freezer-safe containers. Leave room in the containers for the liquid to expand. Thaw the soup overnight in the refrigerator. Do not thaw in the microwave.

To reheat the thawed soup, place it in a microwave-safe dish and microwave on high for 40 to 60 seconds. The dairy products may separate while being heated. Stir the soup well after it is warm to remix the ingredients before eating.

Serves 6

CHIPOTLE SWEET POTATO AND BLACK BEAN CHILI

The sweetness of the sweet potatoes provides a nice balance to the heat of the chipotle seasoning in this vegetarian chili.

I tend to use the orange "yam" sweet potatoes when I make this, but you can use any variety of sweet potato that you have available.

INGREDIENTS

1 tbsp (15 ml) olive oil

1 lb (450 g) sweet potatoes, peeled and diced

1 cup (135 g) diced onion

1 cup (170 g) diced green bell pepper

4 cloves garlic, minced

3 tbsp (27 g) Chipotle Seasoning Mix (page 192)

3½ cups (563 g) fresh diced tomatoes or 2 (15-oz [424-g]) cans diced tomatoes, undrained

3 cups (604 g) cooked black beans or 2 (15-oz [424-g]) cans black beans, drained and rinsed

2 cups (480 ml) vegetable broth

1 green onion, thinly sliced (optional)

DIRECTIONS

Heat the oil in a large pot over medium-high heat. Add the sweet potatoes, onion and bell pepper. Sauté until the onion is translucent, about 5 minutes.

Add the garlic and Chipotle Seasoning Mix to the sweet potatoes. Toss to coat the potatoes and sauté for 1 minute.

Add the diced tomatoes, beans and broth. Stir until thoroughly combined. Bring the chili to a boil. Reduce the heat to low and allow the chili to simmer for 30 minutes, or until the sweet potatoes are fork-tender.

Top with green onion slices before serving.

STORING AND REHEATING

Place the chili in a large covered bowl or individual containers. Store in the refrigerator for up to 5 days or in the freezer for 3 months.

To freeze, ensure the chili has cooled completely then place it in freezer-safe containers. Leave room in the containers for the liquid to expand. If possible, thaw the frozen chili overnight in the refrigerator.

To reheat the thawed chili, place it in a microwave-safe dish and microwave on high for 40 to 60 seconds.

To reheat a frozen bowl of chili, first ensure the container is microwave-safe. Remove the lid and cover the container with a paper towel. Microwave it at 50 percent power for 3 minutes. Continue adding 1 minute at a time until you can stir the chili. Stir the chili to see if it is heated all the way through. If not, microwave on high for 30 to 40 seconds.

WHITE BEAN AND CHICKEN MINESTRONE SOUP

The addition of chicken to this minestrone soup makes it a little more filling for those who don't have time to add a salad and bread to fill up at lunchtime. I don't add pasta to my minestrone because it continues to absorb liquid, and after a couple days in the refrigerator the pasta becomes mushy.

INGREDIENTS

1 tbsp (15 ml) olive oil

1 lb (450 g) boneless, skinless chicken thighs or breasts, cut into bite-size pieces

½ cup (101 g) minced onion

1 medium rib celery, thinly sliced

2 cloves garlic, minced

½ cup (85 g) fresh green beans, cut into small pieces

½ cup (38 g) diced zucchini

⅓ cup (114 g) shredded or julienned carrots

4 cups (960 ml) vegetable or chicken broth

3½ cups (704 g) cooked cannellini beans or 2 (15-oz [424-g]) cans cannellini beans, drained and rinsed

1¾ cups (210 g) fresh diced tomatoes or 1 (15-oz [424-g]) can diced tomatoes, drained

1 tbsp (9 g) Italian Seasoning Mix (page 191)

2 cups (72 g) chopped or shredded kale

DIRECTIONS

Heat the oil in a large pot over medium-high heat. Add the chicken, onion and celery. Sauté for 5 minutes, or until the chicken is browned on all sides.

Add the garlic, green beans, zucchini and carrots to the chicken and sauté for 3 minutes.

Add the broth, beans, tomatoes and Italian Seasoning Mix. Stir until thoroughly combined. Bring the soup to a boil. Reduce the heat to low and simmer for 10 minutes. Add the kale and simmer for 5 minutes.

STORING AND REHEATING

Place the soup in a large covered bowl or individual containers. Store in the refrigerator for up to 5 days or in the freezer for 3 months.

To freeze, ensure the soup has cooled completely then place it in freezer-safe containers. Leave room in the containers for the liquid to expand. If possible, thaw the frozen soup overnight in the refrigerator.

To reheat the thawed soup, place it in a microwave-safe dish and microwave on high for 40 to 60 seconds.

To reheat a frozen bowl of soup, ensure the container is microwave safe. Remove the lid and cover the container with a paper towel. Microwave it at 50 percent power for 3 minutes. Continue adding 1 minute at a time until you can stir the soup. Stir the soup to see if it is heated all the way through. If not, microwave on high for 20 to 30 seconds.

Chapter 8

MAKE-AHEAD DESSERTS

We like to have homemade treats on hand to pack in lunches or for afternoon snacks. I don't mind my kids having dessert as long as it is from scratch and not from a package. This philosophy accidentally set a high bar for what a dessert should taste like to my children, so they naturally limit themselves to desserts made from quality ingredients instead of processed foods.

Limiting my family to homemade treats also limits how many sweets are in the house, because I am going to bake a dessert only a couple times a week—we have to make them last. These make-ahead desserts and snacks all store well and travel well.

CRANBERRY AND WHITE CHOCOLATE CHIP GRANOLA BARS

The chai spices give these cranberry granola bars a unique flavor. Making granola bars is faster and easier than making cookies, so these are a go-to treat when I don't have a lot of time to bake.

INGREDIENTS

½ cup (120 ml) honey

½ cup (90 g) almond butter

3 tbsp (42 g) coconut oil

¼ cup (24 g) almond meal

1½ cups (120 g) old-fashioned rolled oats

¼ cup (30 g) whole flaxseed

2¼ tsp (7 g) Chai Spice Mix (page 189)

½ cup (50 g) dried cranberries

½ cup (90 g) white chocolate chips

DIRECTIONS

Preheat the oven to 350°F (177°C). Grease a 9 x 13-inch (23 x 33-cm) baking dish.

In a small bowl, combine the honey, almond butter and oil. Add the almond meal. Stir in the oats, flaxseed and Chai Spice Mix. Fold in the cranberries and white chocolate chips.

Press the granola into the baking dish. Bake for 20 minutes, or until the edges are golden brown.

Cool completely in the baking dish on a wire rack. After the granola is cool, cut it into 1½ x 4½-inch (4 x 11-cm) bars.

STORING

Store the bars in an airtight container on the counter for 1 week or in the refrigerator for 1 month.

Makes 16

HAZELNUT CHOCOLATE CHIP GRANOLA BARS

Because eating Nutella from a jar is frowned upon, I created a healthier way to combine chocolate and hazelnuts.

INGREDIENTS

½ cup (120 ml) brown rice syrup or honey

½ cup (90 g) sunflower butter

3 tbsp (42 g) coconut oil

¼ cup (21 g) flaxseed meal

1½ cups (120 g) old-fashioned rolled oats

½ cup (80 g) chopped hazelnuts

½ cup (90 g) mini chocolate chips

DIRECTIONS

Preheat the oven to 350°F (177°C). Grease 9 x 13-inch (23 x 33-cm) baking dish.

In a medium mixing bowl, combine the brown rice syrup, sunflower butter and oil. Add the flaxseed meal. Stir in the oats and hazelnuts. Fold in the chocolate chips.

Press the granola into the baking dish. Bake for 20 minutes, or until edges are golden brown.

Let the granola cool completely in the baking dish on a wire rack. After it is cool, cut it into 1½ x 4½-inch (4 x 11-cm) bars.

STORING

Store the bars in an airtight container on the counter for 1 week or in the refrigerator for 1 month.

APPLESAUCE OATMEAL JUMBLE COOKIES

My friend Kathy and her daughter Liz shared their family recipe for Applesauce Jumble cookies with my daughter and me several years ago. The recipe has since gone through several adaptations in my kitchen. No matter which ingredients we "jumble together," every variation has been a hit. If you can't find cinnamon chips, substitute white chocolate chips.

INGREDIENTS

2 cups (250 g) all-purpose flour

¾ cup (60 g) old-fashioned rolled oats

1½ cups (216 g) brown sugar

1 tsp salt

½ tsp baking soda

¾ cup (185 g) applesauce

½ cup (115 g) butter

2 large eggs

1 tsp ground cinnamon

¼ tsp ground cloves

1 tsp vanilla extract

1 cup (121 g) chopped pecans

1 cup (180 g) cinnamon chips, optional

DIRECTIONS

Preheat the oven to 375°F (191°C). Grease 2 (9 x 13-inch [23 x 33-cm]) baking sheets.

In a large bowl, combine the flour, oats, brown sugar, salt, baking soda, applesauce, butter, eggs, cinnamon, cloves, vanilla, pecans and cinnamon chips if desired. Mix well by hand until thoroughly combined.

Drop the cookie dough by level tablespoons onto the baking sheets.

Bake for 10 minutes, or until a cookie bounces back when touched by your finger. Cool the cookies on the baking sheets for 1 to 2 minutes then transfer them to a wire rack to finish cooling.

STORING AND THAWING

Place the cookies in an airtight container. You can store them on the counter for 3 days, in the refrigerator for up to 1 week or in the freezer for 3 months.

Thaw them overnight in the refrigerator. You can place frozen cookies in a lunch box in the morning and they will thaw by lunchtime.

MEXICAN-COCOA COCONUT MACAROONS

Mexican hot chocolate blends a rich chocolate with cinnamon. I have added cinnamon to these chocolate macaroons to capture that unique combination.

INGREDIENTS

1 (14-oz [392-g]) bag sweetened shredded coconut

1 (14-oz [410-ml]) can sweetened condensed milk

½ cup + 1 tbsp (63 g) cocoa powder

3 tbsp (42 g) butter, softened

2 tsp (6 g) ground cinnamon

1 tsp vanilla extract

2 egg whites

DIRECTIONS

Preheat the oven to 325°F (163°F). Line 2 (9 x 13-inch [23 x 33-cm]) cookie sheets with parchment paper.

In a medium bowl, combine the coconut, condensed milk, cocoa powder, butter, cinnamon and vanilla.

In a small bowl, beat the egg whites until peaks form. Gently fold the egg whites into the coconut mixture.

Drop the dough by heaping tablespoons onto the baking sheets. Press the macaroons into a mound shape if necessary.

Bake for 23 to 28 minutes, or until the macaroons are shiny and set. Let them cool on the baking sheets.

STORING AND THAWING

Place the cookies in an airtight container. You can store them on the counter for 3 days, in the refrigerator for up to 1 week or in the freezer for 3 months.

Thaw them overnight in the refrigerator. You can place frozen cookies in a lunch box in the morning and they will thaw by lunchtime.

MOCHA BROWNIE BITES
WITH ESPRESSO BEANS

If you are going to eat sweets in the afternoon, pair them with coffee! These mocha brownie bites are topped with mocha frosting and chocolate-covered espresso beans to make a decadent treat.

MOCHA BROWNIE BITES

½ cup (120 ml) brewed coffee

½ cup (56 g) cocoa powder

1 cup + 2 tbsp (141 g) all-purpose flour

1 tsp baking powder

1 cup (192 g) granulated sugar

⅓ cup (80 ml) mild-tasting oil

1 large egg

1 tsp vanilla extract

MOCHA FROSTING

1 tbsp (14 g) butter

1 tbsp (15 ml) brewed coffee

1 tbsp (7 g) cocoa powder

¼ tsp vanilla extract

Pinch of salt

1 cup (130 g) powdered sugar

36 chocolate-covered espresso beans, for decorating

DIRECTIONS

To make the mocha brownie bites, preheat the oven to 350°F (177°C). Grease mini-muffin pans to make 36 brownie bites.

If the coffee is not already hot, heat it in a small saucepan over medium-high heat until it is hot. In a medium bowl, combine the coffee and cocoa powder. Set aside.

In a large bowl, combine the flour, baking powder and granulated sugar.

Add the oil, egg and vanilla to the cocoa mixture. Stir to thoroughly combine. Add the cocoa mixture to the flour mixture and stir well to combine.

Spoon the batter into the mini-muffin pans. Bake for 10 to 12 minutes, or until a toothpick inserted into the center of a brownie bite comes out clean. Allow the brownie bites to cool completely before frosting.

To make the mocha frosting, combine the butter, coffee, cocoa powder, vanilla and salt in a large mixing bowl. Stir to combine. Slowly add the powdered sugar until it is fully incorporated. Beat the frosting until it is light and fluffy. Add more coffee or sugar to achieve the desired consistency if necessary.

Frost the brownie bites once they are cool then top each one with a chocolate-covered espresso bean.

STORING AND THAWING

Place the brownie bites in an airtight container. You can store them on the counter for 3 days, in the refrigerator for up to 1 week or in the freezer for 3 months.

Thaw the brownie bites overnight in the refrigerator. You can place frozen brownie bites in a lunch box in the morning and they will thaw by lunchtime.

Makes 36

PUMPKIN SNICKERDOODLE BITES

These little muffin bites combine the flavors of two of my favorite cookies: pumpkin and snickerdoodles. Don't leave them unsupervised while cooling or they will disappear.

PUMPKIN SNICKERDOODLE BITES

1 cup (192 g) sugar

⅔ cup (160 ml) mild-tasting oil

1 cup (180 g) pureed pumpkin

1 large egg

1 tsp vanilla extract

2 cups (250 g) all-purpose flour

1 tsp baking powder

½ tsp baking soda

⅛ tsp salt

2¼ tsp (7 g) Pumpkin Pie Spice Mix (page 192)

CINNAMON SUGAR TOPPING

1½ tsp (5 g) ground cinnamon

3 tbsp (36 g) sugar

DIRECTIONS

To make the Pumpkin Snickerdoodle Bites, preheat the oven to 350°F (177°C). Grease mini-muffin pans to make 36 snickerdoodle bites.

In a large bowl, whisk together the sugar and oil. Add the pumpkin, egg and vanilla. Stir well.

In a medium bowl, sift together the flour, baking powder, baking soda, salt and Pumpkin Pie Spice Mix. Add the flour mixture to the pumpkin mixture and mix well.

To make the Cinnamon Sugar Topping, combine the cinnamon and sugar in a small bowl.

Use a cookie-dough scoop to divide the dough between the mini-muffin cups. Sprinkle the cinnamon sugar over the cookie dough.

Bake for 11 to 13 minutes. Place the mini-muffin pans on wire racks to cool.

STORING AND THAWING

Place the bites in an airtight container. You can store them on the counter for 3 days, in the refrigerator for up to 1 week or in the freezer for 3 months.

Thaw them overnight in the refrigerator. You can place frozen bites in a lunch box in the morning and they will thaw by lunchtime.

Makes 12

RASPBERRY-PEAR CRUMBLY CRISP IN MASON JARS

What is the difference between a fruit crisp and a fruit crumble? There really isn't one. I usually call a dessert made with firm fruits (like apples and pears) a crisp and those with soft fruits (like berries) a crumble, so when I pair firm fruits with soft berries, I call it a crumbly crisp.

FILLING

4 medium Bartlett pears or other firm, sweet pears, peeled, cored and diced

2 cups (199 g) fresh raspberries

1 tbsp (15 ml) lemon juice

¼ cup (48 g) granulated sugar

1 tbsp (10 g) cornstarch

1 tsp ground cinnamon

1 tsp ground ginger

TOPPING

1 cup (80 g) old-fashioned rolled oats

½ cup (72 g) brown sugar

¼ cup (38 g) cornstarch

2 tsp (6 g) ground cinnamon

2 tsp (6 g) ground ginger

¼ cup (58 g) cold butter

DIRECTIONS

To make the filling, preheat the oven to 350°F (177°C). Grease 12 widemouthed 8-ounce (240-ml) Mason jars.

In medium bowl, combine the pears, raspberries and lemon juice. Sprinkle the granulated sugar, cornstarch, cinnamon and ginger over the pears and toss to coat well. Divide the pears and raspberries between the jars.

To make the topping, combine the oats, brown sugar, cornstarch, cinnamon and ginger in a small bowl. Cut the butter into the topping mixture with a knife or pastry blender. Sprinkle the topping over the pears and raspberries.

Bake for 20 minutes. Cool the crumbly crisps on a wire rack for 10 to 15 minutes. Serve warm or at room temperature.

STORING AND REHEATING

Place the lids on the jars after they are completely cool. You can store them in the refrigerator for up to 1 week or in the freezer for 3 months.

Thaw them overnight in the refrigerator. You can remove the lid and heat a thawed crisp in the microwave for 30 to 60 seconds.

APPLE-BLUEBERRY
COBBLER IN MASON JARS

My daughter suggested that I add blueberries to my apple cobbler. It turned out to be an incredibly delicious suggestion! This cobbler is topped with a cinnamon biscuit crust, which is easy to make and has a tender and moist crumb.

FILLING

4 medium Fuji apples or other firm, sweet apples, peeled, cored and diced

1 pint (199 g) fresh blueberries

2 tbsp (30 ml) lemon juice

¼ cup (48 g) sugar

1 tbsp (10 g) cornstarch

4 tsp (12 g) Apple Pie Spice Mix (page 189)

TOPPING

1 cup + 2 tbsp (141 g) all-purpose flour

3 tbsp (36 g) sugar

2 tsp (8 g) baking powder

1½ tsp (5 g) ground cinnamon

4 tbsp (56 g) butter

½ cup + 2 tbsp (150 ml) milk

DIRECTIONS

To make the filling, preheat the oven to 350°F (177°C). Grease 12 widemouthed 8-ounce (240-ml) Mason jars.

In a medium bowl, combine the apples, blueberries and lemon juice. Sprinkle the sugar, cornstarch and Apple Pie Spice Mix over the apples and blueberries. Toss to coat well. Divide the apples and blueberries between the jars.

To make the topping, add the flour, sugar, baking powder and cinnamon to a medium bowl. Cut the butter into the flour with a knife or pastry blender until the mixture resembles course crumbs. Slowly add the milk, stirring it into the batter until it is fully incorporated. Spoon the batter on top of the fruit.

Bake for 20 minutes. Cool the cobblers on a wire rack for 10 to 15 minutes. Serve warm or at room temperature.

STORING AND REHEATING

Place the lids on the jars after they are completely cool. You can store them in the refrigerator for up to 1 week or in the freezer for 3 months.

Thaw them overnight in the refrigerator. You can remove the lid and heat a thawed cobbler in the microwave for 30 to 60 seconds.

COOKIES-AND-CREAM CAKE IN MASON JARS

Makes 12

One of my sons has a strong preference for vanilla. The other prefers chocolate. So I call these my "compromise cupcakes."

I use plain chocolate cookies in this recipe. If you use sandwich cookies to make this recipe, scrape out the filling before you crush the cookies. If you leave it in, it will alter the recipe.

By making these cupcakes in canning jars, I can pack them in lunches knowing the frosting won't get smashed.

CAKE

1¼ cups (156 g) all-purpose flour

¾ cup (144 g) granulated sugar

1½ tsp (6 g) baking powder

1 large egg

¾ cup (180 ml) milk

⅓ cup (80 ml) mild-tasting oil

2 tsp (10 ml) vanilla extract

½ cup (80 g) crushed chocolate cookies

FROSTING

⅓ cup (77 g) butter, divided

1½ tsp (8 ml) vanilla extract

Pinch of salt

3 cups (390 g) powdered sugar

2 tbsp (30 ml) milk, divided

⅓ cup (53 g) crushed chocolate cookies

DIRECTIONS

To make the cake, preheat the oven to 350°F (177°C). Grease 12 (8-ounce [240-ml]) Mason jars. Place the jars on a large baking sheet.

In a large bowl, combine the flour, sugar and baking powder.

Beat the egg with a fork. Add the milk, oil and vanilla to the egg. Add the egg mixture to the flour mixture and beat for 2 to 3 minutes on high. Stir in the cookies by hand until fully incorporated in the batter.

Divide the cake batter between the jars. Bake for 20 minutes. Place the jars on a wire rack to cool.

When you place the jars in the oven place the butter in a large mixing bowl. Set the bowl on the counter until the butter reaches room temperature.

When the cupcakes are completely cool, use a mixer, and whip the butter 1 to 2 minutes. Add the vanilla and salt. Mix well. Start adding the powdered sugar 1 cup (130 g) at a time until it is all mixed in.

Add 1 tablespoon (15 ml) of the milk to the frosting then check the consistency. If needed, add the remaining 1 tablespoon (15 ml) of milk until you reach the desired consistency. Whip the frosting mixture for 1 minute. Stir in the cookies. Frost the cakes.

STORING AND THAWING

Place the lids on the jars and store in the refrigerator for up to 1 week or in the freezer for 3 months.

Thaw them overnight in the refrigerator or place a frozen cake in a lunch box and it will be thawed by lunchtime.

UPSIDE-DOWN GERMAN CHOCOLATE CAKES

I make these mini German chocolate cakes in widemouthed 8-ounce (240-ml) canning jars. Instead of frosting the cakes, I mix the coconut and pecans with butter and sugar and spread this on the bottoms of the jars before I add the cake batter. The topping ingredients caramelize while the cakes are baking, creating Upside-Down German Chocolate Cakes.

GERMAN CHOCOLATE CAKE TOPPING

6 tbsp (84 g) butter, melted

6 tbsp (54 g) brown sugar

1¼ cups (7 oz) sweetened shredded coconut

1½ cups (181 g) finely chopped pecans

CAKE

1¾ cups (219 g) all-purpose flour

2 tsp (4 g) baking powder

1¾ cups (335 g) granulated sugar

2 tbsp (30 g) cocoa powder

½ tsp salt

4 oz (113 g) German chocolate

2 large eggs

1 cup (235 ml) milk

½ cup + 1 tbsp (135 ml) mild oil

1 tsp (5 ml) vanilla

DIRECTIONS

Preheat the oven to 350°F (177°C). Grease 12 widemouthed 8-ounce (240-ml) Mason jars.

To make the topping, combine the butter, brown sugar, coconut and pecans. Divide the topping between the 12 jars. Press topping into the jars.

In a large bowl combine the flour, baking powder, sugar, cocoa powder and salt.

Break the German chocolate up into small pieces and place in a microwave-safe bowl. Heat on high for 1 minute. Stir, then heat for an additional minute. Stir, then heat for 30 to 45 seconds, or until the chocolate is completely melted.

Add the eggs to a small bowl. Beat with a fork or egg beater. Add the milk, oil and vanilla to the eggs. Stir to blend.

Add the egg mixture to the flour mixture. Add the German chocolate to the flour mixture and beat on high for 2 minutes.

Divide the batter between the jars. Bake for 33 to 37 minutes, or until a toothpick inserted into the middle of a cake comes out clean.

Place the jars on a wire rack to cool.

STORING AND THAWING

Place the lids on the jars. You can store them in the refrigerator for up to 1 week or in the freezer for 3 months.

Thaw them overnight in the refrigerator or place a frozen cake in a lunch box and the cake will thaw by lunchtime.

Part 3

PANTRY STAPLES

One day, I was picking up ingredients for a cooking class I was teaching. I was in a hurry, so I almost picked up pre-made taco seasoning to use in that day's lesson. I quickly glanced at the label and saw that it contained GMOs. To make matters worse, the genetically modified ingredient wasn't one of the primary ingredients but an unnecessary filler. I changed my lesson plan on the spot and the first thing I taught was how to make seasoning mixes from scratch.

Making spice mixes, sauces and salad dressings from scratch not only gives you complete control over the quality of the ingredients, but saves you money. And it isn't difficult or time-consuming. I have included recipes for pantry staples that you can easily make from scratch to use in the recipes throughout this cookbook.

CHAI SPICE MIX

This Chai Spice Mix has the same delicious flavors that are found in chai tea, minus the tea. My Chai Spice Mix can be used in place of pumpkin pie spice and apple pie spice in recipes. It works well with sweet vegetables and fruits.

Use this spice mix in the Pumpkin-Chai Egg Puffs (page 23), Chai-Spiced Apple Oatmeal (page 70) and Cranberry and White Chocolate Chip Granola Bars (page 168).

INGREDIENTS

4 tbsp (36 g) ground cinnamon

2 tbsp (18 g) ground cardamom

1 tbsp (9 g) ground ginger

1 tbsp (9 g) ground nutmeg

¾ tsp ground cloves

¼ tsp white pepper

DIRECTIONS

In a small bowl, combine the cinnamon, cardamom, ginger, nutmeg, cloves and white pepper. Stir until thoroughly mixed.

STORING

Store the spice mix in an airtight container.

APPLE PIE SPICE MIX

This spice mix makes it easy to make apple pie–flavored recipes. It's used in Apple Pie Baked Oatmeal (page 69).

INGREDIENTS

2 tbsp (18 g) ground cinnamon

1 tbsp (9 g) ground nutmeg

1½ tsp (5 g) ground allspice

½ tsp ground cardamom

DIRECTIONS

In a small bowl, combine the cinnamon, nutmeg, allspice and cardamom. Stir until thoroughly mixed.

STORING

Store the spice mix in an airtight container.

CAJUN SEASONING MIX

Makes ¾ cup (91 g)

This Cajun Seasoning Mix is an easy way to kick recipes up a notch. Although it contains cayenne, the heat does not overwhelm the flavor of the other spices. It is used in the Cajun Egg Croissant Sandwiches (page 35) and Cajun Ranch Chicken and Quinoa Bowls with Chopped Kale (page 102)..

INGREDIENTS

2 tbsp (30 g) salt

2 tbsp (18 g) garlic powder

2 tbsp (18 g) smoked paprika

2 tbsp (18 g) onion powder

1 tbsp (9 g) cayenne

1 tbsp (9 g) coarsely ground pepper

1 tbsp (2 g) dried oregano

1 tbsp (2 g) dried thyme

1½ tsp (5 g) red pepper flakes

DIRECTIONS

In a small bowl, combine the salt, garlic powder, smoked paprika, onion powder, cayenne, pepper, oregano, thyme and red pepper flakes. Stir until thoroughly mixed.

STORING

Store the spice mix in an airtight container.

TACO SEASONING MIX

Makes about ½ cup (61 g)

Taco Seasoning Mix was the first seasoning mix that I started making at home. It just didn't make sense to me to pay for something that contained unnecessary fillers. Use this mix in my Chicken-Fajita Stuffed French Toast (page 51), Turkey Taco Rice Bowl (page 106), Catalina Chicken Taco Pasta Salad (page 126) and Taco Cauliflower-Rice Soup (page 154).

INGREDIENTS

4½ tsp (14 g) chili powder

4½ tsp (14 g) ground cumin

3 tsp (9 g) paprika or smoked paprika

3 tsp (9 g) garlic powder

1½ tsp (5 g) onion powder

1½ tsp (5 g) dried minced onion

1 tsp (1 g) dried cilantro

⅛ tsp cayenne

DIRECTIONS

In a small bowl, combine the chili powder, cumin, paprika, garlic powder, onion powder, dried minced onion, cilantro and cayenne. Stir until thoroughly mixed.

STORING

Store the spice mix in an airtight container.

SEASONED SALT

My friends and family call this "Alea's Seasoning" because I use this seasoned salt recipe in almost every dish I make. In this book, it shows up in many recipes, including the Caprese Egg Cups (page 24), Greek Steak and Lentil Salad (page 122) and Buffalo Ranch Chicken Soup (page 161)—just to name a few!

INGREDIENTS

¼ cup (60 g) sea salt

2 tbsp (4 g) dried parsley

1 tsp onion powder

1 tsp garlic powder

½ tsp dried oregano

½ tsp dried rosemary

½ tsp dried thyme

½ tsp dried sage

½ tsp dried basil

½ tsp dried marjoram

DIRECTIONS

Place the salt, parsley, onion powder, garlic powder, oregano, rosemary, thyme, sage, basil and marjoram in a food processor and pulse until the ingredients are smooth and blended.

STORING

Store the Seasoned Salt in an airtight container.

ITALIAN SEASONING MIX

This Italian Seasoning Mix is just a combination of the herbs and spices most commonly found in Italian dishes. You probably have everything in your pantry that you need to make this seasoning. It's used in the Pizza Breakfast Cups (page 27), Italian Vegetable Mini Frittatas (page 31), Mediterranean Chicken and Vegetable Bowl (page 105), White Bean and Chicken Minestrone Soup (page 165) and Italian Seasoned Croutons (page 197).

INGREDIENTS

2 tbsp (4 g) dried oregano

2 tbsp (4 g) dried basil

2 tbsp (4 g) dried parsley

2 tsp (6 g) garlic powder

1 tsp onion powder

½ tsp dried thyme

½ tsp dried rosemary

DIRECTIONS

In a small bowl, combine the oregano, basil, parsley, garlic powder, onion powder, thyme and rosemary. Stir until thoroughly mixed.

STORING

Store the seasoning in an airtight container.

PUMPKIN PIE SPICE MIX

There is no reason to buy a special jar of pumpkin pie spice when you can make my Pumpkin Pie Spice Mix at home using common pantry staples. Use this spice mix in the Pumpkin Quinoa Muffins (page 63), Overnight Pumpkin Pie–Spiced Pecan Granola (page 74) and Pumpkin Snickerdoodle Bites (page 179).

INGREDIENTS

2 tbsp (18 g) ground cinnamon

2 tsp (6 g) ground nutmeg

2 tsp (6 g) ground ginger

1 tsp ground cloves

DIRECTIONS

Add the cinnamon, nutmeg, ginger and cloves to a spice jar. Put the lid on the jar and shake vigorously to mix.

STORING

Store the spice mix in a lidded container in a cool, dark place.

CHIPOTLE SEASONING MIX

This spicy alternative to taco seasoning is a favorite with my family. It's used in my Chipotle Egg Muffin Sandwiches (page 32) and Chipotle Sweet Potato and Black Bean Chili (page 162).

INGREDIENTS

1 tbsp (9 g) ground chipotle chili pepper

1 tbsp (9 g) garlic powder

1 tbsp (9 g) onion powder

1 tbsp (9 g) ground coriander

2 tsp (6 g) smoked paprika or paprika

1 tsp coarsely ground pepper

1 tsp ground cumin

1 tsp dried oregano (preferably Mexican oregano)

½ tsp Seasoned Salt (page 191)

½ tsp cayenne

DIRECTIONS

In a small bowl, combine the chipotle chili pepper, garlic powder, onion powder, coriander, smoked paprika, pepper, cumin, oregano, Seasoned Salt and cayenne. Stir until thoroughly mixed.

STORING

Store the spice mix in an airtight container.

ITALIAN DRESSING

Make a batch of this dressing to use in side salads throughout the week. It is used in the Ratatouille Grilled Cheese Sandwich (page 151) and Pizza Quinoa Salad (page 129).

INGREDIENTS

1 cup (240 ml) olive oil

¾ cup (180 ml) balsamic vinegar

2 tbsp (30 ml) water

1 tbsp (12 g) sugar

1 tbsp (9 g) dried oregano

1½ tsp (5 g) garlic powder

1½ tsp (5 g) onion powder

½ tsp dried thyme

½ tsp dried basil

¼ tsp coarsely ground pepper

⅛ tsp salt

DIRECTIONS

Combine the oil, vinegar, water, sugar, oregano, garlic powder, onion powder, thyme, basil, pepper and salt in a medium cruet or lidded jar. Shake well to blend the ingredients.

STORING

Store the dressing in a sealed container in the refrigerator for up to 1 week.

RANCH SALAD DRESSING

I can get my kids to eat just about any vegetable as long as I let them dip it in this Ranch Salad Dressing. It is so popular with my family that I have incorporated it in my Cajun Ranch Chicken and Quinoa Bowls with Chopped Kale (page 102) and Chopped Barbecue Pork Salad (page 133).

INGREDIENTS

½ cup (120 ml) milk

1 tbsp (15 ml) lemon juice

¾ cup (91 g) sour cream

1 tbsp (9 g) dried parsley

1 tsp onion powder

¾ tsp garlic powder

½ tsp dried dill

½ tsp dried basil

½ tsp Seasoned Salt (page 191)

¼ tsp ground mustard

¼ tsp coarsely ground pepper

DIRECTIONS

In a small bowl, combine the milk and lemon juice. Let this mixture sit for 5 minutes.

In a small bowl, combine the sour cream, parsley, onion powder, garlic powder, dill, basil, Seasoned Salt, mustard and pepper. Mix well to combine.

Add the milk mixture to the sour cream mixture and blend well.

Refrigerate the dressing in an airtight container for 1 to 2 hours before using.

STORING
Store the dressing in a sealed container in the refrigerator for up to 3 days.

Makes 3½ cups (840 ml)

SPAGHETTI SAUCE

Homemade spaghetti sauce is easy to make and can be made in the time than it takes to cook pasta. This recipe is used in the Zucchini Parmesan Bowl with Spaghetti Squash (page 110).

INGREDIENTS

1 tbsp (15 ml) olive oil

½ cup (68 g) diced onion

4 cloves garlic, minced

1¾ cups fresh diced tomatoes or 1 (15-oz [424-g]) can diced tomatoes, undrained

1¾ cups tomato sauce or 1 (15-oz [450-ml]) can tomato sauce

1 tbsp (12 g) sugar

1 tbsp (9 g) Italian Seasoning Mix (page 191)

DIRECTIONS

Heat the oil in a large saucepan over medium-high heat. Add the onion and garlic. Sauté for 5 minutes, or until onion is tender.

Add the tomatoes, tomato sauce, sugar and Italian Seasoning Mix. Stir to combine.

Bring the sauce to a boil. Reduce the heat to low and simmer, uncovered, for at least 15 minutes.

STORING

Store the sauce in an airtight container in the refrigerator for up to 5 days or in the freezer for up to 1 month.

Makes 1½ cups (360 ml)

PIZZA SAUCE

Pizza sauce is another sauce that is easy to make at home. Use it in the Pizza Breakfast Cups (page 27).

INGREDIENTS

1 (15-oz [450-ml]) can tomato sauce

2 tsp (2 g) dried oregano

1 tsp dried thyme

1 tsp dried basil

1 tsp garlic powder

1 tsp onion powder

2 tsp (8 g) sugar

¼ tsp Seasoned Salt (page 191)

Dash of coarsely ground pepper

DIRECTIONS

In a small saucepan over medium-high heat, combine the tomato sauce, oregano, thyme, basil, garlic powder, onion powder, sugar, Seasoned Salt and pepper. Bring the sauce to a boil.

Reduce the heat to low and simmer for 10 minutes.

STORING

Store the sauce in an airtight container in the refrigerator for up to 1 week or the freezer for up to 3 months.

BARBECUE SAUCE

While this sauce is delicious in any barbecue recipe, I love to use it in my Chopped Barbecue Pork Salad (page 133).

INGREDIENTS

1¾ cups tomato sauce or 1 (15-oz [450-ml]) can tomato sauce

2 tbsp (30 ml) apple cider vinegar

¼ cup (36 g) brown sugar

2 tbsp (30 ml) maple syrup

2 tbsp (30 ml) Worcestershire sauce

2 tsp (6 g) garlic powder

2 tsp (6 g) onion powder

1½ tsp (5 g) ground mustard

1 tsp chili powder

½ tsp ground cinnamon

¼ tsp red pepper flakes

DIRECTIONS

In a medium saucepan over medium-high heat, combine the tomato sauce, vinegar, brown sugar, maple syrup, Worcestershire sauce, garlic powder, onion powder, ground mustard, chili powder, cinnamon and red pepper flakes. Bring the mixture to a boil.

Reduce the heat to low and simmer for 15 minutes.

STORING

Store the sauce in an airtight container in the refrigerator for 1 week or the freezer for up to 3 months.

ITALIAN SEASONED CROUTONS

I usually make these croutons with sandwich bread, but you can make croutons with any leftover pieces of bread that you have on hand. Make a batch to enjoy on side salads or in the Zucchini Parmesan Bowl with Spaghetti Squash (page 110).

INGREDIENTS

8 to 10 slices sandwich bread

¼ cup (60 ml) olive oil

1 tsp (9 g) Italian Seasoning Mix (page 191)

DIRECTIONS

Preheat the oven to 450°F (232°C).

Place the bread on a large ungreased baking sheet. Brush one side of the bread with the oil and dust it with the Italian Seasoning Mix. Repeat the process on the other side of the bread.

Using a pizza cutter, cut the bread up into bite-size pieces.

Bake for 5 to 8 minutes, or until the croutons are toasted and brown, tossing the every 2 to 3 minutes.

Leave the croutons on the baking sheet to cool.

STORING

Store the croutons in an airtight container on the counter for 5 days or in the freezer for up to 1 month.

CARAMEL SAUCE

Makes 1¼ cups (300 ml)

Caramel sauce is actually pretty quick and easy to make at home, so I usually do (especially since it is hard to find store-bought caramel sauce that doesn't contain high-fructose corn syrup).

Use this homemade indulgence in Caramelized Pear Slow Cooker Oatmeal (page 77).

INGREDIENTS

1 cup (144 g) brown sugar

½ cup (115 g) butter

½ cup (1220 ml) heavy whipping cream

Pinch of salt

½ tsp vanilla extract

DIRECTIONS

In a medium saucepan over medium heat, combine the brown sugar, butter, cream and salt. Bring the mixture to a boil and cook for 2 minutes, stirring occasionally.

Remove the saucepan from the heat and stir in the vanilla. Let the sauce sit for a couple of minutes to cool.

STORING

Store the sauce in an airtight container in the refrigerator for up to 2 weeks.

BLUEBERRY SYRUP

Makes 2 cups (480 ml)

You can make real blueberry syrup quite easily if you wish. This syrup can be served over Lemon Chia Seed Waffles (page 44).

INGREDIENTS

1 cup (240 ml) blueberry juice or water, divided

1 tbsp (10 g) cornstarch

2 cups (199 g) frozen blueberries, thawed

⅓ cup (64 g) sugar

DIRECTIONS

In a small bowl, whisk together ¼ cup (60 ml) of the blueberry juice and the cornstarch until the ingredients are thoroughly combined and lump-free.

In a medium saucepan over medium-high heat, combine the blueberries, the remaining ¾ cup (180 ml) of blueberry juice and the sugar. Stir to combine. Cook until the mixture reaches a boil. Reduce the heat to medium-low, stir in the cornstarch mixture, and simmer for 7 minutes, or until the mixture thickens.

Carefully use either a blender or an immersion blender to puree the blueberries. If your family does not like the chopped-up bits in the syrup, you can pour it through a sieve before serving.

STORING

Store the syrup in an airtight container for up to 1 week in the refrigerator.

APPLE CINNAMON SYRUP

This is a frugal and delicious alternative to maple syrup. This can be used on the Peaches and Cream Stuffed French Toast (page 52).

INGREDIENTS

1 tsp ground cinnamon

⅛ tsp salt

3 tbsp + 1½ tsp (35 g) cornstarch

1⅔ cups (400 ml) water

1 (12-oz [350-ml]) can apple juice concentrate, thawed

1 tsp vanilla extract

DIRECTIONS

In a small saucepan over medium heat, combine the cinnamon, salt and cornstarch. Gradually stir in the water and apple juice concentrate until the mixture is smooth.

Cook, stirring frequently, until the mixture begins to boil. Reduce the heat to medium-low and cook at a low boil, stirring continuously, for 2 minutes, or until the syrup thickens.

Remove the syrup from the heat. Stir in the vanilla. Serve warm.

STORING

Store the syrup in an airtight container in the refrigerator for up to 1 week.

ACKNOWLEDGMENTS

The day I announced that I finished my last cookbook, my sister Corriedawn asked, "When are you going to write a breakfast and lunch cookbook?" This book started to take shape in response to her "push." I will forever miss her enthusiastic encouragement.

Thank you to the Page Street Publishing team for providing me a platform to share my prep-ahead recipes. Marissa, Meg B. and Laura G., I appreciate your input and guidance in pulling this book together.

I am grateful to Ken Goodman for travelling to Nevada to photograph the recipes in my home. Ken, thank you for taking charge of the plating and food styling. You did an amazing job capturing the flavors of my recipes in your photos.

I am thankful to everyone who helped keep Premeditated Leftovers running while I was busy developing recipes. Christine, Emily, Patricia, Anjanette Y., Katie F., Jody, Grant, Katie H., Tatanisha and Derrick, I sincerely appreciate your contributions to the blog.

I appreciate the encouragement and support I have received from my blogging friends Cris, Dana, Kim, Taylor, Amy, Tricia H., Rebecca P. and Wendy.

I am thankful to my parents for encouraging my creativity in the kitchen when I showed an interest as a child and to my mother-in-law for taking me under her wing after I married her son.

Thank you to my friends and neighbors who served as taste testers. The Chapelle family has gone above and beyond in providing feedback on my recipes, carefully noting cooking times. Pauline and Maralee not only regularly serve as guinea pigs for my recipes, they organized the packaging and delivery of all of the food that was cooked during the cookbook photoshoot, ensuring that none of the food went to waste.

A huge thank-you to my friend Rebecca L., who flew out to help me cook all 75 recipes in 4 days for the photoshoot. It was every bit as hard as I thought it would be and I would not have been able to pull it off without your help!

A special thank-you to my family for their willingness to accompany me on this crazy journey.

Patricia, cooking is always a more joyful experience when you are in the kitchen! Thank you for sharing your ideas and providing feedback despite your busy schedule.

Grant, your enthusiasm for the recipes and the concept was motivating! It was encouraging to see how the recipes fit into your schedule and fitness goals.

Andrew, you have become an amazing sous chef! I enjoy your company and appreciate your help in the kitchen.

Pete, thank you for your support, for the countless runs to the grocery store, for trying to keep up with the never-ending sink of dirty dishes and for helping me carve out time to create and write.

ABOUT THE AUTHOR

Alea Milham is the author of *Prep-Ahead Meals from Scratch.* She is also the founder of the food blog Premeditated Leftovers, where she shares simple recipes made with whole foods, practical shopping tips, time-saving techniques, ideas for minimizing food waste and meal-planning strategies.

While volunteering as a budget counselor, Alea recognized that food is the element of most people's budgets over which they have the greatest control. She set out to develop low-cost, from-scratch recipes so her readers could create delicious meals on a limited budget. She realizes that eating well while spending less is about more than just creating recipes using inexpensive ingredients; it's about creatively combining ingredients so you don't feel deprived and are inspired to stick to your budget.

Alea lives on two acres in the high desert with her husband, children and small menagerie. Her favorite hobby, gardening, is a frugal source of organic produce for her recipes.

INDEX

Lemon Chia Seed Waffles, 44
Peaches and Cream Stuffed French Toast, 52
Peanut Butter Chocolate Chip Blender Pancakes, 43
Pumpkin Quinoa Muffins, 63
Ranch Salad Dressing, 194
Strawberry Rhubarb Baked Oatmeal, 66
Upside-Down German Chocolate Cakes, 187
milk, almond
Chocolate Peanut Butter Overnight Oatmeal, 73
Gingerbread Overnight Oatmeal, 73
Peaches and Cream Overnight Oatmeal, 73
milk, cashew, for Chocolate Peanut Butter Overnight Oatmeal, 73
milk, chocolate, for Chocolate Peanut Butter Overnight Oatmeal, 73
milk, powdered
Blueberry-Walnut Oatmeal, 70
Chai-Spiced Apple Oatmeal, 70
Cinnamon Spice Oatmeal, 70
Mocha Brownie Bites with Espresso Beans, 176
molasses, for Gingerbread Overnight Oatmeal, 73
Mongolian Beef and Broccoli Bowl, 98
Monterey Jack cheese
Chicken-Fajita Stuffed French Toast, 51
Chimichurri Steak Breakfast Burrito, 39
Chipotle Egg Muffin Sandwiches, 32
Jalapeño Chicken Pita Pockets, 143
Jalapeño Corn Bread Waffles, 47
Southwestern Chicken Salad Lettuce Wrap, 148
Taco Cauliflower-Rice Soup, 154
Turkey Taco Rice Bowl, 106
mozzarella cheese
Caprese Egg Cups, 24
Caprese Spaghetti Squash Bowl, 114
Honey Mustard Ham and Cheese Quesadillas with Broccoli, 144
Italian Vegetable Mini Frittatas, 31
Pizza Breakfast Cups, 27
Pizza Quinoa Salad, 129
Zucchini Parmesan Bowl with Spaghetti Squash, 110
muffins
Chai-Spiced Carrot Cake Muffins, 60
Chocolate Hazelnut Muffins, 59
Hummingbird Zucchini Muffins, 56
Pumpkin Quinoa Muffins, 63
mushrooms
Chicken Marsala Pocket, 140
Greek Steak and Eggs Pita Pockets, 36
Hearty Steak and Mushroom Stew, 158
Italian Vegetable Mini Frittatas, 31
Pizza Quinoa Salad, 129

Salad Bar Vegetable Salad, 130
Sherry Pork with Bacon and Brussels Sprouts, 113
mushrooms, portobello, for Ratatouille Grilled Cheese Sandwich, 151
mustard
Greek Quinoa, 91
Greek Steak and Lentil Salad, 122
Ham and Cheese Ranch Drop Biscuits, 55
Honey Mustard Ham and Cheese Quesadillas with Broccoli, 144
Lemon-Dijon Chicken Pasta Salad, 121
Mediterranean Chicken and Vegetable Bowl, 105
Ranch Salad Dressing, 194
Salad Bar Vegetable Salad, 130
Salmon-Berry Quinoa Bowl, 109

oat flour
Blueberry-Walnut Oatmeal, 70
Chai-Spiced Apple Oatmeal, 70
Cinnamon Spice Oatmeal, 70
Peanut Butter Chocolate Chip Blender Pancakes, 43
oats
Apple Pie Baked Oatmeal, 69
Applesauce Oatmeal Jumble Cookies, 172
Blueberry-Walnut Oatmeal, 70
Caramelized Pear Slow Cooker Oatmeal, 77
Chai-Spiced Apple Oatmeal, 70
Chai-Spiced Carrot Cake Muffins, 60
Chocolate Peanut Butter Overnight Oatmeal, 73
Cinnamon Roll Slow Cooker Oatmeal, 78
Cinnamon Spice Oatmeal, 70
Cranberry and White Chocolate Chip Granola Bars, 168
Gingerbread Overnight Oatmeal, 73
Hazelnut Chocolate Chip Granola Bars, 171
Hummingbird Zucchini Muffins, 56
Oatmeal Packets, 70
Overnight Pumpkin Pie–Spiced Pecan Granola, 74
Overnight Refrigerator Oatmeal, 73
Peaches and Cream Overnight Oatmeal, 73
Raspberry-Pear Crumbly Crisp in Mason Jars, 180
Strawberry Rhubarb Baked Oatmeal, 66
olives, black
Greek Steak and Eggs Pita Pockets, 36
Greek Steak and Lentil Salad, 122
Mediterranean Chicken and Vegetable Bowl, 105
Pizza Quinoa Salad, 129
onions
Asian Chicken Quinoa Salad, 125
Batch-Cooked Mason Jar Eggs, 19
Batch-Cooked, Ovenbaked Scrambled Eggs, 16

Batch-Cooked Sheet Pan Eggs, 20
Bourbon Beef and Quinoa Bowl, 101
Buffalo Ranch Chicken Soup, 161
Cajun Ranch Chicken and Quinoa Bowls with Chopped Kale, 102
Carrot Soup with Lentils, 157
Chimichurri Steak Breakfast Burrito, 39
Chipotle Egg Muffin Sandwiches, 32
Chipotle Sweet Potato and Black Bean Chili, 162
Chopped Chimichurri Steak Salad, 118
French Dip Grilled Cheese Sandwich, 136
Hearty Steak and Mushroom Stew, 158
Italian Vegetable Mini Frittatas, 31
Mongolian Beef and Broccoli Bowl, 98
Pizza Breakfast Cups, 27
Southwestern Chicken Salad Lettuce Wrap, 148
Spaghetti Sauce, 195
Taco Cauliflower-Rice Soup, 154
Taco Seasoning Mix, 190
Turkey Taco Rice Bowl, 106
White Bean and Chicken Minestrone Soup, 165
onions, green
Chipotle Sweet Potato and Black Bean Chili, 162
Chopped Barbecue Pork Salad, 133
Garlic and Rosemary Sweet Potato Pancakes, 48
Ham and Broccoli Mini Quiche with Hash Brown Crust, 28
Honey Mustard Ham and Cheese Quesadillas with Broccoli, 144
Jalapeño Chicken Pita Pockets, 143
Jalapeño Corn Bread Waffles, 47
Lemon-Dijon Chicken Pasta Salad, 121
Pizza Breakfast Cups, 27
Vegetable Fried Cauliflower Rice, 88
onions, red
Cajun Egg Croissant Sandwiches, 35
Catalina Chicken Taco Pasta Salad, 126
Chicken-Fajita Stuffed French Toast, 51
Chimichurri Steak Breakfast Burrito, 39
Chopped Chimichurri Steak Salad, 118
Greek Steak and Eggs Pita Pockets, 36
Greek Steak and Lentil Salad, 122
Mediterranean Chicken and Vegetable Bowl, 105
Pizza Quinoa Salad, 129
Ratatouille Grilled Cheese Sandwich, 151
Salad Bar Vegetable Salad, 130
Sherry Pork with Bacon and Brussels Sprouts, 113
orange juice, for Vegetable Fried Cauliflower Rice, 88
Overnight Pumpkin Pie–Spiced Pecan Granola, 74
Overnight Refrigerator Oatmeal, 73